A LOVELY LITTLE WAR

Life in a Japanese Prison Camp
Through the Eyes of a Child

By

Angus M. Lorenzen

Published in the United States by
History Publishing Company
Palisades, New York

Library of Congress Cataloging-in-Publication Data
Lorenzen, Angus M., 1935–
    A Lovely Little War/Angus M. Lorenzen.
    —1st ed.
    p.cm.
    LCCN 2008926741
    ISBN-13: 978-1-933909-13-4
    SAN: 850-5942

Printed in the United States on acid-free paper
9 8 7 6 5 4 3 2 1

First Edition

DEDICATION

It is the children of Santo Tomas who carry the lantern today that continues to light that dark time so long ago when war and deprivation was all we knew. We survived, although so many others did not. But we survived only because our parents sacrificed to shield us from the dearth, uncertainty, and horror that they knew. And so this book is dedicated to all of the parents in the Santo Tomas Internment Camp, many of whom had to hold their families together in the absence of a husband or wife who died or was carried away by the Japanese, some never to be seen again. I especially dedicate it to my mother, Elsie Farquharson Lorenzen, who lost the prime of her life, but never her humor and dedication. To all of the parents, we salute you!

CONTENTS

FOREWORD

When direct occupants in a war are children, their lives are changed forever. Some do not make it. There are more of us, in unity, alive today, who have traveled that same path. I too, along with many others, know this first hand. The American–Civilian experience during WWII in the Philippines is a one of a kind, unique part of our history. I might add, it is an experience over 63 years old, which is just now gaining national attention.

So please, listen to this child's voice. It is pure and perceptive beyond years. It gives the reader a child's innocent thoughts and recognition of a hot war he personally witnessed in a Japanese prison camp. His pre-war life as a boy in England and China tells the story of privilege and adventure. Woven with the realities of danger and episodes of humor, the boy, Angus Lorenzen, brings us all to that delicious climax—Liberation! And the wonders of Freedom! The man, Angus Lorenzen, still remembers, but moves on.

—Sascha Jean Weinzheimer Jansen

Sascha Jansen, who was a prisoner in the Santo Tomas Internment Camp, is the narrator of events in Manila during World War II in the Ken Burns documentary, The War. She is the primary force in the ex-prisoner community in keeping alive their history for their descendents and the greater community.

ACKNOWLEDGMENTS

An author's ego may lead him to the belief that his book is the result of only his inspiration and perspiration. In truth, it is a team effort with many others contributing to the product, so I thank my team and acknowledge their efforts. Foremost is Joan Paris, who took on the challenge of reading each chapter as it was completed, hit me on the head when I got out of line, and asked the questions that forced me to reconsider what I was trying to say.

Sascha Jean Jansen is the glue that keeps we ex-prisoners from the Philippines connected, and is the organizer of that fabulous trip to Manila for the 60th anniversary of the liberation. It was then that I became inspired to write this book as I met and exchanged stories with others who were prisoners, GIs who liberated our camps, Filipino guerillas, and military POWs who suffered through the horrors of the Bataan Death March and camps like O'Donnell, Cabanatuan, and Bilibid.

Lou Gopal accompanied us on that trip and filmed the narratives of many ex-prisoners, most of whom were children in those dark years. His documentary *Victims of Circumstance* provides additional perspectives and added details that I had all but forgotten. He also generously provided photos from his archival research.

The book written by Frederick H. Stevens and published in 1946, *Santo Tomas Internment Camp*, was exceptionally valuable because it provided a diary that firmly fixed when various events happened, specific dates that I could never have remembered. He was one of our camp leaders, and keeping the records hidden from the Japanese searches was a challenge that risked his being jailed, beaten, or perhaps sharing the fate of other leaders who were executed.

Last, but not least, are the folks at History Publishing Company who accepted the challenge of publishing this book. Specifically, I thank Don Bracken for seeing something worthwhile in the manuscript that arrived over the transom at his office and Tom Cameron for his editing efforts that tightened the story and smoothed the prose.

PROLOGUE

It was February 3, 2005, and I was an honored guest of the University of Santo Tomas in Manila. Earlier in the day, I had attended a number of ceremonies, including the opening of a museum exhibit of the years the University was used by the Japanese as a concentration camp, and I had spoken to a packed audience at a colloquium for students and faculty who were unaware of what horrors had occurred within their beloved campus. Now I was seated in the plaza where a sumptuous banquet was being served and the University orchestra was playing American and Filipino classics. The University president, the American Ambassador, and a Filipino senator had made their stirring speeches, and we could now relax and enjoy the balmy evening.

As the sky darkened to a pink afterglow, the façade of the Main Building of the University, adjacent to the plaza, was lighted with multi-colored fairy lights, almost replicating the way the sky was lighted by flares on a similar evening 60 years earlier. The rumble of the orchestra's kettledrums was like that deep rumble that permeated the air those many years ago.

I looked at my watch, and at 8:30 I turned to the Filipino gentleman named Diosdado Guaytingco who sat next to me and said, "60 years ago to this minute, I was sitting in the hallway of the third floor up there," I pointed upward at the nearby Main Building. "I was savoring the remaining crumbs of our last survival biscuit wondering what would come first, death or rescue." I looked at him expectantly, hoping to hear his story.

"I was outside of the main gate," he pointed in that direction, "tending to my dying leader." He had been in the lead jeep that was guiding the 44th Tank Battalion flying column to the gates of Santo Tomas with orders to make a daring rescue before the Japanese could execute us. On that exact day 60 years earlier, I was 9-years-old and Disdado was 22.

Moments later on that long-ago evening, a tank named "Battlin' Basic" reared back and crashed through the wall into the campus. Along with the rest of the tanks and vehicles, Diosdado followed with a litter carrying the mortally wounded Captain Manuel Colayco, who had met the 800-man column at the outskirts of Manila and guided it through the Japanese defenses. Both he and the American battalion commander had been wounded in a skirmish with the Japanese at the gate, but they had met their mission's objective.

When the cavalry arrived to rescue us, I, along with most of the other prisoners, started wildly celebrating our liberation. However, the battle inside our camp was not yet over. Throughout Manila, it was just the beginning of what turned out to be the fiercest urban battle fought by American forces in World War II, resulting in a staggering number of casualties. We were about to witness the total destruction of a city.

The warm feelings I felt that evening in 2005 reflected on our freedom after more than three years as prisoners, and the ceremonies on the campus were a celebration of the sixtieth anniversary of the liberation. They were also a reminder of the horrible toll that the city suffered in its aftermath.

But why was I in what was then known as the Santo Tomas Internment Camp in 1945? War has a strange way of bending one's life, causing things to happen that you never plan nor expect. I was in England on that late August day in 1939 when the European conflict that escalated into World War II began. And from that day on, the winds of war blew me half way around the world and then back again.

I was a child, and children view war differently from adults. Think of pictures you have seen of children playing in a bomb-blasted neighborhood when the battle has briefly passed. You see what appear to be carefree individuals, and can't imagine what horror they may have recently faced. You see them happily gather around soldiers, who become their heroes and role models. They haven't yet developed the life experience that eventually will lead them to hate and fear war.

So now I tell my story of those war years from the viewpoint of a child, with the light moments and humor that are a big part of a child's life. In all its agony of blood, death, and destruction, the war is seen through a prism that distorts the harsh light into a colorful spectrum, and only towards the end does it break through to focus on the deadly events that came to be known as the "Battle of Manila."

ONE

HOPE FROM THE SKY

February 3, 1945, dawned as just another dreary day, my 1,125th as a prisoner in the Santo Tomas Internment Camp. I dragged myself off the wooden pallet that was my bed and pulled on my ragged shorts, the standard uniform of the day without shoes or shirt. Pulling back the mosquito net that provided the only privacy in the dormitory, I stepped into the crowded aisle and headed for the hallway, scratching at the welts caused by the ubiquitous bed bugs that had been gnawing at my flesh during the night.

My only thought was to get to the breakfast line and put some food into my rumbling and complaining stomach. I went down the stairs from the third floor of the Main Building to the lobby on the ground floor, then out through the large rear door into the street beyond. It was here that the communal outdoor kitchen had been set up, and as early as I was, there was already a long line of hungry people waiting for their scoop of watery lugao.

I waited in line as patiently as a 9-year-old boy could, but to tell the truth, none of us had any energy for horsing around, and we stood as placidly as a row of cows. Finally it was my turn at the serving counter, and I lifted my tin cup for the server to put in a scoop of lugao. The serving had been the same size for a long time, almost filling my cup. But over the last year as food supplies diminished, water had increasingly become the largest ingredient, and the few grains of swollen rice sank to the bottom of the cup.

I carefully carried my cup to our shanty, which was only a couple of hundred yards away, and sat in a chair to slowly spoon the mixture into my mouth. By eating very slowly, it seemed to allay the pangs of hunger. Soon my mother and sister, who also had carried their cups to our private space, joined me and followed the same procedure of delicately eating their fare. The process was an illusion, because as soon as we finished we were hungry again, and there would not be another meal until 5 o'clock in the afternoon.

It was soon time for the morning roll call, and we walked wearily back to the Main Building and painfully up the two flights of stairs to the third floor. Now came another ritual that was designed to humiliate us. Twice a day everyone from our dormitory was required to line up in two rows along the wall in the hallway. As the Japanese officer and his guards approached down the hallway, the room monitor called out, "One, two, three, bow," and we all performed the practiced bow, feet together, arms pressed to our sides, and bent perpendicular at the waist. If the bow wasn't perfect, one or more of us could earn a cuff on the head, or in extreme cases, the butt of a rifle in the gut. We held the bow until the room monitor had reported all present and accounted for, and the group of Japanese moved down the hallway to the next dormitory.

We remained at our roll call station until the PA system announced that we were dismissed. Today that came quite quickly, indicating that the Japanese were not taking any special precautions, such as looking for a potentially escaped prisoner or searching dormitories for contraband articles such as electrical appliances or written journals. Sometimes we were kept at our roll call stations for three or more hours at a time. When dismissed today, the three of us returned to our shanty where we had a modicum of privacy to read, knit, or nap. We had little energy to do anything else.

Late in the morning I heard an aircraft approaching. I was now very familiar with the sound of aircraft and could identify the type, and often the mission, from the sound. Most recently we had been seeing American P-47 and P-51 fighters on bombing and strafing missions close by, sometimes just beyond the walls of the camp. The engines of these high-performance aircraft had a mean growl that turned into a scream as they dived towards their targets. But the sound of this aircraft was different. I went into the open outside of our shanty to see what it was.

Coming from the north at treetop level, flying low and slow was a Marine Corps SBD Douglas Dauntless dive-bomber. It flew by so close that I could see the pilot and gunner clearly through their open canopies. I waved frantically as it went by, though had a Japanese guard seen me, I would have been severely punished. The pilot grinned and waved back. Then the dive-bomber flew over the Main Building and disappeared.

It was only a matter of minutes afterwards that word rapidly spread through the camp. The gunner had dropped his goggles with a note attached that said, "Roll out the barrel." This was a sign of hope because it is the first line of a song that ends, "For the gang's all here." We knew that the American forces were close, but had no idea where they were, or when they would arrive to rescue us. Now the prisoners saw a gleam of hope, and smiles appeared on many faces that had been glum for too long.

In the afternoon, two more SBD dive-bombers flew over at low altitude, but no more messages were dropped, which was probably a good thing because if the Japanese suspected that they were, more people might be arrested and disappear. Already four of our camp leaders had been taken away and were never again seen alive, and the camp's head doctor had been jailed for refusing to change starvation as the cause of death on the numerous death certificates our doctors had to prepare daily. Since the start of American bombing raids the last September, the Japanese administration of the camp had become increasingly harsh, and even the smallest infraction of their rules was treated with prison time and beatings.

Finally, dinner time arrived. I was in line with my tin cup half an hour before the 5:00 start of serving. My mother and sister joined me in the line, and when we got our scoop of stew, we carried it back to our shanty to enjoy our dinner. Stew was the sardonic appellation we gave to what at best could be called a soup. It consisted of a few leaves of talinum, a green-leafed plant grown in the camp garden, floating on top of a watery broth with a few beans at the bottom. Our habit was to slowly spoon up the greens and broth until only the beans remained, then to count the beans and eat each one individually until it completely dissolved in our mouth. That afternoon, I had eight beans.

After dinner, we returned to our dormitory and repeated the ritual for evening roll call. Again, the guards seemed unconcerned, and we were dismissed in a relatively short time. But if the guards were so unconcerned, why were we building such a head of excitement? Surely if the American forces were nearby, the Japanese guards would be taking unusual precautions to defend themselves and the camp, and wouldn't behave as if it was business as usual. We had heard rumors that the Japanese would execute all prisoners before allowing the American forces to rescue us, and perhaps their behavior was simply intended to keep us calm until they could carry out their plan.

After roll call, I went to the washroom near the rear entrance to the Main Building. I showered in the cold water and brushed my teeth then went outside to enjoy the balmy evening before returning to the dormitory at curfew. The sun had set, but a rosy glow remained in the sky, silhouetting columns of smoke in several places outside the camp. From time-to-time, I could hear explosions and gunfire, but we were now so accustomed to this, as a result of the constant bombings, that we paid scant attention.

As the sky grew darker, I could see a strange fluctuating glow that appeared and then disappeared at various points around the northern horizon. I could hear a low-frequency rumble. It was not so much heard as felt in the chest. Perhaps this was another portent, as was the message this morning of imminent rescue, and I became very excited.

At curfew, I returned to the third floor of the Main Building to join my mother and sister where they were sitting at a card table in the hall outside of our dormitory. My mother brought out the precious tin box in which she kept the survival biscuits she had made with the corned beef from our Red Cross package for Christmas of 1943 and from black-market soy meal she had bought at that time. She had baked the biscuits in a clay oven until they were dry and hard so they would keep in the humid atmosphere. She called them hardtack.

She opened the box and took out one of the two remaining biscuits that were all that stood between survival and starvation. She carefully broke the biscuit into three pieces, evenly dividing the crumbs between us. We sat, sucking on the small pieces, savoring every moment as they slowly dissolved and trickled down our throats. Soon everything was gone, and that hollow feeling returned to our stomachs.

Then my mother did something totally uncharacteristic for someone who had shown such care and thrift for the last three years. She opened the box again and took out the last biscuit. As she shared it into three pieces she said, "What the heck, this will all be over very soon anyway." Whatever happened in the next day or two, whether we were rescued or massacred, we wouldn't need the survival biscuits any longer.

But how did we get into this situation in the first place? It was half a lifetime ago when we had been carefree and happily enjoying our holiday with my grandparents in the north of England when Germany invaded Poland, starting World War II. I remember how excited I was that there would be a real war in my lifetime, something very different from the make believe wars that my little lead soldiers fought on the living room carpet. How had things turned so wrong? How had we been catapulted from our life of ease and privilege into the maelstrom of war half a world away, a war whose bitterest events we were yet to see and feel?

TWO

INTRODUCTION TO WAR

The sun broke from behind a bank of puffy white clouds as I careened down the gravel path on the small, wheeled cart propelled by a bevy of laughing children. As I neared the terrace where the adults were sitting, I turned the steering handle hard to the left. The cart turned over, spewing me out onto the gravel with the tiny bodies of the other children tumbling on top of me. We lay in a tangled pile giggling and wiggling while the adults jumped up and raced over to see how badly damaged we were.

I had achieved my purpose, which was to gain the attention of the adults. They picked me up and dusted me off, soothing the tiny scratches and abrasions. When they were finally assured that no lasting damage was done, I strutted around with my legion of tiny cohorts, glorying in the attention.

I deserved the attention. It was my birthday, August 13, 1939, and the party was being held to celebrate this momentous occasion when I reached the significant age of four. I was the youngest of the children present, who included my sister, Lucy, and the two daughters of my Uncle Ian. I was fair-haired, sharp nosed, with a somewhat receding chin and dark blue eyes with slightly down-turned eyelids that could make me look quite soulful when that was my desire. And that was a device I employed quite frequently to get my own way. I thought I was most handsome because that is what my parents and Amah my

Chinese nursemaid told me. Although looking at those early photos, I might now disagree.

On this beautiful late summer day, we weren't in Tientsin, China, which was my family's home, but at the Garlands Institution for the Insane in Cumberland near the Scottish border where my mother had been brought up. Her father was a medical doctor and headed the institution, so we kids had free run of the expansive gardens. My mother, sister, and I had been here for almost three months on home leave; in another two weeks, we would be boarding a luxury liner to head home to China.

But calling attention to ourselves at just that moment was exactly the wrong thing to do, because once the adults were reassured that we would survive our tumble, we were banished to our rooms for a nap. The grown ups had serious things to discuss, and they were not for little ears.

∞ ∞ ∞

It seemed like there had been lots of serious discussions among the adults this summer, and we children had been shooed away when we tried to listen. Children are perceptive, and it seemed to me as if the mood in the household had taken a major downturn in the last few weeks. Compared to earlier in our holiday, the adults didn't seem to be as happy and carefree, and the number of excursions and day trips away from the insane asylum had been greatly reduced. Even Uncle Ronald, who had a great joy for life and was a notable prankster, seemed subdued. And Uncle Ian, an officer in the Royal Navy, had been called back to duty before his holiday was over, leaving his wife, Aunt Jane, and my two cousins to remain with us until the end of August.

I realize now that the shadow that started to darken our holiday that summer was the events that led to the start of World War II. We had booked passage for the end of August on the *SS Rawalpindi*, one of the great P&O liners that made the Asia run from England. The sudden cancellation of our travel plans was my first indication that all was not well in the world, because we stayed with my grandparents well past our planned departure date. I was very disturbed because I had so been looking forward to the exciting trip home. When I tried to get an explanation for the delay, my mother simply dodged my questions.

I didn't find out until a few days later, from my sister, that on September 3, Britain and France had declared war on Germany because of some nasty man called Hitler. Lucy found out when she overheard the servants talking about one of the gardener's assistants leaving to join the army so he could fight in the war. Years later I found out that the luxury liner, to my great disappointment, had been requisitioned by the Royal Navy, fitted out as a merchant warship, and renamed *HMS Rawalpindi.* She had been fitted with 6-inch guns, and was on picket duty near Iceland when she encountered a pair of German battle cruisers and engaged them to delay their attack on the convoys. With their superior firepower, the German cruisers soon sank the *Rawalpindi,* but she had done enough damage to the German ships that they had to return to port for repairs. The loss of *Rawalpindi* is one of the most heroic naval sacrifices of World War II.

Anyway, it was exciting news to find out that we were at war. A lovely little war would be much more fun than some trip on an old luxury liner! I didn't realize it then, but I had been living in a war zone already for two years of my life. I was only two years old when Japan declared war on China. Within days, the Japanese had bombed Tientsin, where I lived, and then invaded and occupied the city along with a large swath of coastal China. Perhaps that was really the start of the Second World War, though our Euro-centric culture always places it as the German invasion of Poland in 1939.

But by the time I was old enough to be cognizant of such things, the Japanese and Chinese were fighting elsewhere, and our patch of North China was quiet. Not only was it quiet, but also seemingly secure and well run. No longer did we foreigners have to worry about rampaging warlords and incursions by the Kuomintang. The Japanese administered the city in a thoroughly organized manner that largely left the foreign concessions unaffected. At my young age, I never realized that I was living in a Japanese occupied city.

To me, war was what happened when I set up my little lead soldiers to do battle on the living room floor. The brave Scots in their blazing red coats and kilts stood shoulder to shoulder facing the Zulus in South Africa, and though many were knocked down, they always won the day. Then they would be put away in their box until they could fight another day against the Sepoy mutineers in India or the rampaging Boxers in China.

These were the stories that my mother told me, based on the heroic battles of the British Empire that she had learned when she was a child. My attitude might have been different had the war stories been told by my father. He served with the American Expeditionary Force in France during the Great War and received a battlefield commission, which is how he became an American citizen. And the coming World War would follow more closely the widespread scourge that he knew rather than the neat little battles of my mother's history books and my fantasies.

∞ ∞ ∞

Our stay at the insane asylum stretched another two months. It was no longer summer, the days were getting short and the overcast and rain were more frequent as the temperature cooled. It wasn't just the weather that was gloomy. The gloom also descended over the entire household.

Britain was mobilizing, men were being recruited into the services, and trained troops were being sent to France to defend against a German invasion. But all was quiet on the fields of Belgium, Holland, and France as the German army attacked to the east into Poland. The major action affecting Britain was on the high seas where German battle cruisers and U-boats started a campaign to sink the ships providing the lifeline to the British Isles. Within hours after war was declared, a U-boat sank the British liner *SS Athenia* bound for America with 1,100 civilians aboard. The danger of trying to return to China under such circumstances was clear to my mother and grandparents, if not to me.

Then Uncle Ronald came up with a brilliant solution. As shipping manager for Imperial Chemical Industries, he possessed a great deal of knowledge about, and influence over, the ships bound in to and out of Britain. He arranged our passage on a Japanese ship called *Haruna Maru*. Japan had signed a friendship agreement with Germany, and it was unlikely that a German U-boat would attack a friendly nation. Also, because of the Japanese interests in Tientsin, the ship would sail directly to our home city without requiring us to change ships in Hong Kong or Shanghai as might have been required on a British ship.

As October neared its end, my grandfather drove us into Carlisle, the nearest city from the asylum, and we boarded a train for the half-day trip to Liverpool. Uncle Ronald was standing on the platform when the train arrived at the Liverpool station, with two porters and a baggage trolley. He looked so big and fierce with his round face and mustache, a tall heavyset, fun-loving man like my father.

Uncle Ronald quickly organized the porters to handle our luggage, taking it out of the baggage car and loading it onto the trolley. When traveling by ship in those days, people were inclined to take great volumes of luggage, at least one steamer trunk per person along with several suitcases. On the luxury liners that plied the routes to China, first-class passengers dressed formally for dinner each evening, plus they needed many changes of clothing for daytime and for excursions ashore. In addition, my mother had purchased clothing and sundries while in England, which she might not be able to readily obtain in China. Though we were not returning on a luxury liner, we were still well loaded down with luggage.

Sitting at the curb outside the station was Uncle Ronald's large touring car into which we were ushered. As large as this vehicle was, there was no chance that the luggage would fit, so Uncle Ronald set about hiring a couple of taxis to convey the luggage to dockside, giving the drivers explicit instructions where they were to go. Uncle Ronald jumped into the driver's seat of his chariot, and we soon arrived dockside on the Mersey River where our transport awaited.

My attention immediately focused on the ship, for though it was a freighter of modest means, it seemed enormous to me as I stood on the dock and gazed upward and along the sweep of its deck from stem to stern. Cranes were loading nets filled with cargo into her holds both fore and aft. Great gangs of stevedores were on the dock working at a leisurely pace loading crates in the nets and positioning and hooking the crane cables to the cargo going aboard. It was a peaceful scene, with other ships at the docks also loading and unloading, and that made it difficult to believe that a war was going on. Nobody seemed to have any sense of urgency, and there was no sign that some of the ships at nearby docks had arrived in convoys, braving attack in the North Atlantic, and others would soon be outbound into those same dangerous waters.

The war was yet young, and though German U-boats and heavy cruisers threatened the convoys, the amount of shipping was only a fraction of what it would become as the war progressed and the Germans strived terribly to cut off the lifeline that kept Britain alive and a threat to German dominance in Europe. The next time I saw these same docks, six years later, they were reduced to rubble by the blitz the Germans had launched against this great shipping port.

We climbed up the gangway to the deck, where an English-speaking Japanese officer met us. He led us up a stairway inside the central island of the ship and showed us a large accommodating cabin that had a single bed, a pair of bunk beds, and several pieces of furniture. Cabins in many passenger/freighters were much larger and more comfortable than what we have learned to expect today on modern cruise ships. But then, we expected to be aboard the ship for a month, and a cramped cabin would have made it a rather uncomfortable voyage.

An announcement, made in English and Japanese, instructed all visitors to proceed ashore, and we made our last farewells with Uncle Ronald. My mother's were particularly emotional, which I didn't really understand because she was not a particularly emotional person. But I suspected that Uncle Ronald was her favorite brother, outgoing, full of fun and jokes, and the instigator of her trip to visit his family eight years earlier when he lived in Tientsin. It was there that he introduced her to his good friend Max Lorenzen, the man she would later marry and who became my father. Her other brother, Ian, was a Commander in the Royal Navy and seemed to me more austere and restrained, like my grandfather. I learned when I was older that he had a wonderfully subtle and wry sense of humor, but that wasn't apparent to me as a child.

∞ ∞ ∞

Uncle Ronald descended the gangway and stood on the dock as the lines were cast off. He waved enthusiastically as the ship moved away from the dock and into the roads to pass downriver and into the ocean. We were now truly off, and as the lights of the city disappeared astern, we were called to dinner.

We had a table to ourselves while Japanese businessmen, along with a few other Western couples who were lucky enough to get accommodations for their return to China, occupied the other tables. My mother seemed relieved to see the other Westerners because she'd have people with whom to spend time, since Westerners and Japanese did not mix well socially. I was disappointed, though, because there were no other children aboard, which meant I'd get stuck with only my bossy sister as a playmate.

Over the next few days, we developed a routine of playing, eating, and napping that made the days pass. Occasionally there were interesting sights to see, like the day we passed through the Straits of Gibraltar and could see the British fortress on one side and Africa on the other. There was no clue at that time of the intense German bombing that was soon to make life miserable for the British defending this important stronghold controlling access to the Mediterranean.

Eventually, we arrived at our first port—Marseille—a big French city on the Mediterranean. The ship was only staying a day to load some additional cargo, so my mother decided that we only had time to explore the port area on foot. After being confined in such a small space for the past few days, we certainly needed the exercise.

This was still the period called the Phony War in Europe, where Germany was not yet threatening its other Northern European neighbors as it and its ally, the Soviet Union, voraciously consumed Poland. Life in Marseille seemed as relaxed as it had in Liverpool, with no outward sign that anyone was concerned about the war that soon was to devastate their country. The sleek light-gray warships of the French Navy that were docked nearby fascinated me. It was hard to believe that within another year France would surrender to Germany and the British would sink the French fleet.

We survived our little shore excursion, and my mother eagerly awaited our next port of call—Naples. Italy had not yet joined its German ally in declaring war on Britain and France.

When we arrived, we could see Mount Vesuvius dominating the skyline. My mother hired a guide with a car to take us to Potsuoli near the base of the volcano. Here we explored the lava fields and fumaroles, and our guide showed us that the heat coming out of the ground was hot enough to ignite a rolled-up newspaper. The Italians were a happy, friendly people, but little did we know that even then they were planning to declare war on Britain and would soon be engaged in bitter warfare in North Africa.

∞ ∞ ∞

Naples was the last stop to load cargo on our voyage, and we now proceeded directly to Tientsin. This was the longest leg of our voyage, but along the way we went through the Suez Canal. I loved this part of the trip because we seemed to glide across the desert, and occasionally we'd see Arabs riding on camels, just like in my picture books. Soon the canal would become the focal point in Germany's North Africa campaign, and the British desperately defended it to prevent this vital link to her African and Asian colonies from falling into German hands.

After leaving the Suez Canal, we were mainly at sea with just the occasional glimpse of land. Time seemed to drag forever during this part of the trip, and to make it worse, my mother started to teach me to read. I was not a willing student, but she had a captive audience, and I had little choice but to go along with the lessons. By the end of this period of intensive training, I could read and write simple sentences, and actually enjoyed my new-found ability.

After we passed Singapore and turned north, the weather turned more temperate and became much more comfortable. Soon we passed the coast of North China and entered what could be called virtually a Japanese sea. As a result of the war on the Chinese government they instigated in 1937, the Japanese occupied most of the coast of China, as well as Taiwan, Korea, and Manchuria. When we entered the Yellow Sea, Japanese-occupied lands surrounded us, with Korea to the east, Manchuria to the north, the Shantung Peninsula to the south, and Tientsin and North China to the west.

∞ ∞ ∞

We arrived off the town of Taku, where the Peiho River empties into the sea, just about noon, then moved slowly up the Peiho for several miles, finally arriving at the docks in Tientsin late in the afternoon.

Now I was really in a dither to get off the ship, see my father, and get back to the home from which I'd been absent for six months. We were all packed with the luggage in our cabin ready to be taken ashore, but now came one of the most frustrating things I can remember. We were not allowed to disembark from the ship. The purser explained that the Japanese authorities ashore had to process all of the ship's papers before we could land, and they would not be able to do it until the next day.

We resigned ourselves to another night aboard ship, or at least my mother did because I was very cranky about the situation. When dinner was called, we went to the dining room. Strangely, it was practically empty except for our table and those of the other Westerners. All of the Japanese businessmen were gone. My mother asked our waiter why they weren't dining, and he said that they had all gone ashore. Holding the Westerners aboard was harassment imposed by the Japanese occupation forces that would become more intense as Japan consolidated its holdings in Asia and diplomatic relations with the West deteriorated. We were helpless to do anything in the face of this deliberate bureaucratic roadblock.

We were just about finished with dinner when my father came bounding into the dining room. His presence was unmistakable because he was so large and had such a commanding presence. I jumped off my chair and ran to him, and he swept me into his arms and kissed me, much to my embarrassment. My mother and sister joined me and after hugs and kisses all around, my mother asked the key questions. How did he get aboard and what was he doing here?

He said that he was here to take us home. When my mother protested that the Japanese authorities wouldn't let us go ashore, he laughed, and said he knew someone in the military command who took care of everything. In later years, I realized that my father had paid a bribe, *cumshaw* in the Chinese idiom, which was completely within his character and not uncommon in the way business was done in China. I was elated. At last we got to leave the *Haruna Maru* and its large white flag with the big red circle in the center waving from its stern. More importantly, we were home in a place where I was pampered and content and nothing bad could happen.

THREE

A BRIEF IDYLL

The next two years, from 1940 through 1941, were a period of privilege and contentment for me at home in Tientsin. I remember them as being among the best years of my life. The war in Europe turned vicious, but it was a long way away. As a child, I was unaffected by the worries my mother had for her family in England. I just lived for the pleasures of the moment. But by the end of this period, big things were clearly afoot in Asia. People there were much more aware than people in America that we were on the brink of war with Japan. Many were leaving for safe havens, and the Philippine Commonwealth was considered to be one of them because it was part of America and because a large military force was maintained to protect the islands.

In later years, people have asked why we didn't leave China while we had the chance, if it was so obvious that war was about to break out. They could ask the same question of people who live on an earthquake fault or in a tornado alley, and the answer would be the same. People are tied to the land that is their home, and hope is eternal that when disaster strikes, they will be spared.

My father lived virtually all of his life in China. In many ways he was more Chinese than American. Leaving China was unthinkable to him. And when circumstances finally forced him to leave permanently after the war, he always yearned to return, though that was impossible for an American citizen. As it turned out, remaining in China after hostilities with Japan started would have been a better choice for us than what eventually happened.

∞ ∞ ∞

Our home in Tientsin was in the British concession, the largest of the eight or so foreign concessions in the city. It was on a quiet street lined with large homes. Ours was two-stories with a full basement reached by a narrow, steep stairway that led down to the kitchen, storage areas, and servants' quarters. On the first floor was a large living room, a dining room that could comfortably seat 20 people, and other general rooms for entertaining. Our bedrooms were upstairs. Off my parent's room was a large screened porch where they kept canaries, frequently opening the cage doors to let them fly free around the porch.

In front of the house was a well-manicured front lawn, with a driveway and garage on the side of the house. The back yard— a great playground—was lush, expansive, and surrounded by a high wall that separated it from our neighbors on all sides. Most of this space was lawn, and along the back was a vegetable garden. On one side was a cold flat flush with the ground where vegetables and lettuce could be grown in the cooler months, with glass windowpane lift-up doors. Now, in late November 1939, the lawn and most of the garden were covered with a thick layer of straw to keep the plants safe from the bitter winter. Tientsin was fairly far north, only 90 miles from the old Chinese capital of Peking, which was not far from the edge of the Gobi desert.

My father, Max Andreas Lorenzen, was North China Manager for American Asiatic Underwriters, which was part of the insurance company that later became AIG. He had lived in Tientsin most of his life, from the time when he moved from his birthplace in Newchwang to start school. He was the child of a Danish sailing ship captain and his wife who were shipwrecked in Chinese waters in the 1880s. He had only been away from China for a short period of his life during the Great War. When that war broke out in 1914, he was living in the German concession, where the British confined him until he tried to escape to get back to his job working for an American company. The British guards shot him in the thigh, then shipped him off to Australia to a POW camp. His American friends got him paroled, and he arrived in the United States shortly before America declared war on Germany in 1917. He promptly joined the Army and was shipped to France at the end of 1917. Serving as a First Sergeant and top kick of his unit, he received a battlefield commission and with it his U.S. citizenship. After the armistice, he was stationed in Germany with the occupation forces. During this time, he married an American nurse. When they returned to Tientsin, he had been away for four years.

His first wife died during a typhus epidemic. Their son, my half brother, was several years older than my sister and me. My mother, Elsie (Farquharson) Lorenzen, had lived at the asylum in England for most of her life until my Uncle Ronald came home on leave and persuaded my grandparents to pay her way out to China for a visit with he and his wife. At the time, Uncle Ronald was North China Manager for Imperial Chemical Industries and lived in Tientsin. Reluctantly, my grandfather agreed, and when my mother arrived, Uncle Ronald introduced her to his good friend Max. She never returned to Cumberland except for short home visits. They married that same year, and after a respectable time, my sister came along, and a couple of years later so did I.

My father, a big wheel in the city, knew almost everyone, or at least those of any importance. He possessed a verve for life: full of humor, generous to a fault, and with an outgoing personality. In addition to his position with American Asiatic Underwriters, he was a bank director, a consultant to the Chinese government, and had many acquaintances in both the Chinese and Western business communities. He was Post Commander of the American Legion. When the U.S. 15th infantry was stationed in Tientsin, before President Roosevelt pulled them out in 1937 to avoid a confrontation with the Japanese, he became an intimate with many young officers who later became the leading American generals during World War II. One of those officers, Dwight David Eisenhower, became supreme commander of allied forces in Europe during World War II and later was elected President of the United States.

My father still maintained contact with the Marine contingent stationed in Tientsin, which was responsible for guarding the consulate in this city as well as the embassy in Peking. He also knew most of the people in the American and British consulates, so he was well tapped into the political sectors of the community.

My mother, an athletic woman, took Tientsin by storm. She became a champion golfer, tennis player, and bowler. Our home was littered with silver cups, ashtrays, and other trophies engraved with her name and accomplishments. She also liked to accompany my father on hunting trips, taking her fair share of birds using a lighter shotgun than my father used.

My sister, Lucy, was two and one-half years older than me, and typical of older sisters, was bossy and overbearing. She was born in Tientsin, and my father immediately registered her birth with the American consulate, so she was an American citizen. I was born in England when my mother made a home visit four years after she had moved to China. I think she wanted one of her children to be a British citizen, which is why she took the trip at that time. But my father also registered my birth at the American consulate, so I had the option of British or American citizenship when I grew up. At that time, I was going to a British school and had many British friends, so I was leaning in that direction.

We were members of the Episcopal Church in Tientsin, as were many of the expatriate Westerners. How we became Episcopalian I can't say, but our family album has baptism pictures at the church's font for both my sister and me, each of us probably wailing like banshees. My mother's father was from the Highlands of Scotland. He probably was brought up in some stern and uncompromising Calvinistic religion. Thank God she didn't choose to follow in his footsteps. Her mother was a Quaker, and I'm sure if we had taken up her religion, we would have had a difficult time turning the other cheek during subsequent events.

My father, who had an abiding hatred for missionaries of any stripe, went along with whatever religion my mother chose and probably avoided the services as frequently as he could. But my mother made sure we attended services and went to Sunday school. I'm not sure how strong her faith was, but she lost all of it when we almost lost our lives as Japanese prisoners. Many years later when we were living in California, I remember her being approached by a religious zealot while she was working in the garden. After he inquired politely about the faith to which she belonged, she replied that she didn't have any faith. That set him off on a rant about her need to find Jesus or else she would be condemned to eternal hell. She looked at him with steely eyes, and replied, "I've already been in hell and nothing your God promises holds any fear for me." He looked shocked, then tucked his bible and pamphlets under his arm and slunk away, while my father stood on the porch roaring with laughter.

Though I thought she was bossy, the truth is that Lucy and I got along well and only suffered from the normal sibling rivalries. My half-brother, John, was a lot older and was going to a boarding school in Peking. I only got to see him on holidays and vacations, but when he was home, he made us the center of attention and was a lot of fun.

We were members of the country club, which had a large indoor swimming pool that I loved, plus boating on the lakes during summer and ice-skating during winter. The club also had the requisite golf course, tennis courts, and bowling greens where my mother could demonstrate her athletic prowess. And the club was the center of social life for the Western community, with parties, dinners, and balls.

It was especially nice for me, because my father was very indulgent and let me have almost anything I wanted. My mother was stricter, but I could work my wiles with either Amah or my father to get around any strictures that she might make. I felt comfortable at school and made friends with many of my classmates, and even had a girl friend, a little girl name Heather. My time was completely filled with parties, family outings, and sports. If ever I felt bored, I could hang out with the servants, who might feed me a special treat or take me for an excursion into the Chinese part of the city.

My parents entertained a great deal, and my sister and I were usually exiled from these galas. But anytime he entertained his Chinese friends or associates, my father would bring my sister and me to meet the visitors. There was terrific benefit to this custom because the visitors would always bring a gift for us. It would be a boat, or train, or some other toy suitable for a boy. Both my sister and I would get the exact same gift, which would greatly upset her because she would much have preferred a doll. My father explained that the Chinese revered boys, so they always favored them, but this did not mollify my sister in any way, and she'd leave the room pouting.

My father also coached me in saying, "Gung shi, gung shi fa tsi," which he said meant happy New Year. Of course, my father was a great joker, and I might just as well have been saying, "Alms for the poor". Anyway, when I used this expression with his Chinese friends, they always dug into their pockets and gave me some coins. What a bonanza! I would use this expression all year long, not just during our own or the Chinese New Year periods, and after a hearty laugh, the visitors would always cough up some loot for me. I figured that I'd be independently wealthy by the time I was seven, not realizing that the small coins I was collecting were only worth a fraction of a penny.

∞ ∞ ∞

We lived a comfortable, happy, and privileged life. That war hung over us may have worried the adults, but to us kids, it was a remote thing that didn't significantly affect our lives. Oh, there were war-oriented activities, even for the kids. My mother sponsored circles with her friends to cut and roll bandages to send to

England for the wounded, and my sister and I often participated. Also, there was a big drive to collect tinfoil, which was used to package candy, tobacco and cigarettes, to be sent to help the war effort. We rolled the tinfoil into balls, and there were competitions to see who could create the biggest and heaviest ball. I was usually the champ because both my parents smoked, but more importantly, my father put the arm on his friends to bring us their foil, and my collection grew at an amazing rate.

We children really didn't have any idea how the war was going far away in Europe; but by the spring of 1940, the German blitzkrieg was sweeping through the Low Countries into France, forcing the British army against the Channel coast. It seemed as if the British would lose a large part of their defensive force but for what Prime Minister Churchill called the miracle of Dunkirk. The picture became increasingly grim as Italy declared war, France surrendered, and the lifeline to the colonies through the Suez Canal was threatened. German submarines were sinking a huge number of ships in the convoys bringing supplies from America, and Germany started bombing London and other cities. Then the German armies started massing along the Channel Coast, preparing to invade England itself.

But of more significance to us was when Walt Disney's first feature length animated movie, *Snow White and the Seven Dwarfs,* arrived in the Tientsin movie theater. Soon we kids were singing our own version of the dwarfs' signature song.

Whistle while you work,
Whistle while you work.
Hitler's barmy,
So's his army,
Whistle while you work.

We also sang bastardized versions of popular military songs from World War I, such as:

You're in the army now,
You're not behind the plow.
You'll never get rich,
You son of a bitch.
You're in the army now.

The first time my mother heard that song, she banned us from singing it again. She wasn't going to have children in her home using bad words. I appealed to my father, and he suggested that we use some other term for the one that offended my mother. I asked if he had any ideas, but the best he could come up with was, "Son of a sea cook." I suppose because of his nautical heritage, he thought that was a suitably disparaging term, but it sure didn't work in the song. Eventually, someone came up with, "Son of a witch", and because it was satisfactory to everyone, we went back to singing our song.

∞ ∞ ∞

The days passed as eventfully as they could for me, carrying the burden of a full and satisfying life, and soon it was summer of 1941. My brother, John, came home from school for the holidays, and our home was in turmoil from his exuberant romping and new games for my sister and me.

For the summer, my parents rented a cottage on the beach at Peitaho, just a short distance north of the city of Chingwandao, the next major city up the coast. There were numerous cottages sprinkled along the top of the dunes behind the beach, which was washed by the Yellow Sea. Western families who wanted to get away from the mid-summer heat of Tientsin and Peking stayed in them. My mother and we kids spent the whole summer, while my father remained in Tientsin and came up on the train on many of the weekends. John was with us most of the summer. Little did we realize at the time that this carefree summer would be the last one we would ever spend together as a family.

∞ ∞ ∞

When Autumn arrived, we returned to Tientsin. I had responsibilities and had to return to my British-style school, which was much more rigorous than the school the Americans attended. I missed John terribly when he left our household to go to Shanghai and college. He had changed from a tall, gangly youth to a confident young adult. As light hearted and impetuous as he was, our home seemed emptier without him. He was passing from childhood to adulthood, and the gap in time before I would once more see him created a gulf that would never again be closed. He had survived childhood, but in the months ahead, he would take such great risks that the penalty for failure would be execution.

The war was not going well for Britain, and though the children were insulated from the bad news that continually depressed our parents, we knew that something was not right. Where were my dreams of glory on the battlefield? They were shattered by the lack of any meaningful victories for our side. Because of the grim situation, our parents told us practically nothing, and we children had a difficult time getting excited about a war of which we knew so little. The older children in the community were able to glean more information, but the stories that filtered back down the line were not at all satisfying.

As 1941 wore to a close, a frenetic round of parties and dances served to distract adults and children alike. There was a reason for all the frantic activity. It was a badly kept secret that the Japanese were on the verge of attacking American interests in Asia and declaring war. The Japanese already occupied a large part of China, all of French Indo China, and were allied with Siam, so they had a good foothold in Asia. But they hungered for the riches of Burma, Malaya, the Dutch East Indies, New Guinea, and Borneo. They knew that the British and Americans would not let them freely take these territories. The British, already weak in Asia because they had committed so many of their resources to the European war, were of little threat to them. But America had repeatedly warned against any further adventurism by Japan, thus the answer had to be a massive surprise attack on the Americans to prevent them from resisting the Japanese ambitions. Bettors were making book that the start of the war would be a Japanese surprise attack on the Philippines.

Knowing that war was imminent, by December 1941 most American diplomats had been evacuated from the Japanese occupied cities in China. In Tientsin, the U.S. Marine contingent was packing its equipment and heavy weapons, and had chartered a ship to depart on December 12 to transport them to the Philippines. The British diplomatic corps announced that it would stay, but their intelligence informed them that Japanese troop ships were hovering off the Malay Peninsula, and some reports indicated that Japanese troops were already going ashore in some remote areas. Could there be any question in the minds of the Western community about what was in store for them?

The summer of 1941 was the last happy time for Angus and Lucy before war disrupted their lives.

FOUR

A FAREWELL TO CHINA

December 1941 arrived with a cold snap and icy winds blowing from the direction of the Gobi Desert in the north. Our garden was again covered in straw to insulate it, and my mother had dug out our winter clothing so that I also was well-insulated in woolen clothing, gloves, and an aviator-style cap. School was more challenging now that I had started to become more advanced in reading and writing. In arithmetic, I was starting to learn long division.

I hated long division, considering it just too difficult for a six-year-old to have to accept. I clearly remember one particular evening in early December. My mother and I were in the living room of our home sitting at a small table while she tried to coach me through the intricacies of long division. I was in a bad mood and resisted her every effort. I don't know what my mental block was, for later in life I progressed in mathematics through calculus, differential equations, Fourier series, and LaPlace transforms; but that particular evening, I just was not willing to put my mind to solving math problems. Being both strong-willed and spoiled, I did not make it easy for my mother.

My father walked into the living room and broke up the lesson, much to my relief. He needed to talk to my mother in private. I wound up going to the basement kitchen where our cook gave me a treat. It was something I definitely didn't deserve for my behavior, but I wasn't going to tell cook that, particularly when she was so willing to indulge me.

Later in the evening after dinner, my mother took my sister and me upstairs and told us we needed to pack. We were going, she said, to Hong Kong to spend the Christmas holidays and would be leaving tomorrow. What about John and my father? Were we not going to be with them for Christmas? Oh yes, of course we would all be together for Christmas. They would join us in Hong Kong shortly before the holiday, since my father had to take care of business and John was very busy with his college courses.

The conditions seemed perfect for a grand holiday season, and we were going to a place with a much nicer winter climate. Best of all, I'd get out of school a couple of weeks early. I was elated to be able to dodge the lesson time, particularly in long division. I set to with a will to help my mother pack a suitcase for me. Any niggling concerns that I might have had over this trip, which was so out of character for my parents, were overridden by my excitement about doing something new. Not until years later did I realize we were not leaving for a special holiday but were fleeing Japanese occupied Tientsin in the face of imminent war.

The next afternoon, we set off for the docks in my father's chauffer-driven car. With only one suitcase apiece, we had not packed as if we were taking a luxury liner back to Europe. Time had just not allowed us to pack up the large steamer trunks. If we had, I think I'd have been more suspicious of our intent.

When we arrived at the Peiho River, we drove to the coal-loading dock where a small ship was docked. My father told me that it was called a *collier* because it transported coal. The ground was black with spilled coal dust, but the holds of the ship were already filled and the decks scrubbed down, so there was little opportunity for me to get thoroughly blackened before we were in the passenger space. The island on the ship was fairly small. Two passenger cabins were at deck level, and the dining salon the next deck up. The navigation bridge, just forward of the salon, opened on to the dining room. We could see the helm and the ocean through the windows of the enclosed bridge. An open flying bridge, with extensions to each side, was above the enclosed bridge.

Only four passengers were aboard, the three of us in one cabin and a lady named Mrs. Costain in the other. She was about the same age as my mother and also came from the north country of England, either Cumberland or Yorkshire. The two of them had much in common. As for me, I was stuck with either my sister as a playmate or had to use my own resources, for which there were many opportunities under the loose administration of our captain.

When we arrived, the ship was already prepared to leave. The captain was waiting until the tide was right to sail across the Taku bar at the mouth of the river. Shortly after we settled into our cabin, the steward came by and told us the ship was ready to sail, and my father should go ashore.

The three of us went onto the deck as my father strode down the sloping gangway to the dock where he stood, a lone observer of our departure, as the hawsers were taken in and a tug nudged the ship slowly away. We stood on deck, bundled in coats against the frigid wind, waving as the ship started down river. He became smaller and smaller as the distance increased, a lonely figure rooted to the land where he grew up, as we disappeared around a bend in the river. It didn't concern me that we were leaving him behind because in only two weeks he would join us in Hong Kong. But little did I know that I would not see my father again for six years. When we did rejoin, we were both very different people.

∞ ∞ ∞

The voyage was a delight for me. I had the run of the ship. The officers and crew were exceptionally pleasant, answering my million questions, and letting me explore the nooks and crannies, including the engine room. The officers were British and the crew was primarily Chinese. Though its cargo was coal, it was all sacked and stored within the holds, and the rest of the ship was kept scrubbed and clean. Still, I managed to get completely black with coal dust every time I made a new excursion, and my mother kept busy directing me into the bathtub for a thorough scrubbing from stem to stern.

Rather than sail through the straits that separated Formosa from the mainland, the captain decided to stay east of the island in open ocean. Though I didn't know the reason at the time, it was because of the imminent threat of Japanese attack. The Japanese occupied both sides of the narrow straits, and if war started, the ship might be trapped. This turned out to have a negative consequence, though, which delayed our arrival date in Hong Kong by half a day.

A typhoon swept into the East China Sea just to the north of our position. Late in the afternoon, the winds rose and the ocean became turbulent. The ship started to roll and pitch as if it were riding on the back of an enormous bucking bronco. I thought this was great fun as we staggered from the dining salon, where we had just finished dinner, to our cabin. As we went down the stairs and along the companionway, I let my self bounce from wall to wall, giggling the whole time. By this time, we had all gained our sea legs, and motion sickness was not a problem. But to play cards or board games required a stable platform.

That evening, my mother sent us to bed early. I was again in the top bunk, and as I wrapped the covers around me, I could feel myself roll from one side of the bed to the other. I was quite enjoying the sensation when I fell asleep. Not long after, I was rudely awakened when I rolled completely out of bed and tumbled to the cabin floor. My mother jumped up, panicked that I'd been hurt, but it was nothing, and I laughed and said I'd like to try it again. My mother didn't accept that. She searched around and found a railing that could be put up on the open side of the bed. That kept me safe for the rest of the night.

Sometime during the small hours of the morning, I awoke to the drip of cold water on my bed. My loud complaint awakened my mother, who turned on the light and discovered water was dripping from the ventilator in the ceiling. She rang for the steward, who stumbled in a few minutes later in a state of disarray as he had been jolted from his own sleep. He examined the problem and told us that in the rough sea and driving rain water was getting into the ventilator funnels on deck and running down the duct to our cabin. He stuffed some towels into the ventilator to soak up the water and promised the problem would be corrected in the morning. Since my bed was now soaking wet, my mother moved me down to the lower berth with my sister. We slept end-to-end for the rest of the night.

By morning, the storm had passed and the ship's routine returned to normal. It was Sunday. We had expected to arrive in Hong Kong that evening, but the storm delayed us, and we now would arrive early the next morning. As it turned out, the result of this delay would save us from a very unfortunate situation.

∞ ∞ ∞

Monday morning, at an earlier than expected hour, the steward knocked on our door and told us that the captain had requested that we assemble in the salon. It was still dark. My mother also acted a little puzzled. When I asked why we were getting up so early, she said it was probably something about the formalities involved in landing in Hong Kong. We got dressed and soon were in the salon where we met Mrs. Costain. She too was responding to the captain's request.

The captain soon joined us. My mother and Mrs. Costain were quite disturbed at what he had to say. I didn't really understand it all, but it sounded like a good news, bad news situation. Just a couple of hours earlier on the other side of the International Date Line where the calendar was a day earlier than ours, Japanese bombers had attacked the American fleet in Pearl Harbor. For them, it was Sunday, December 7. The good news was that the expansion of the war had finally started. Now the Americans would put the Japanese in their proper place, since they had been a thorn in our side for as long as I could remember.

∞ ∞ ∞

As our ship passed the outer islands and entered Hong Kong harbor, we noticed unusual activity with the other shipping. A steady stream of ships sailed past us, outbound from the harbor, and other ships were pulling up their anchors and preparing to depart. All Allied ships were leaving Hong Kong as fast as they could get up steam and make way.

Our ship proceeded in an orderly fashion to its berth at the coal docks on the Kowloon side of the harbor and tied up by 9 o'clock. As soon as it was possible to go ashore, my mother hustled us down the gangway and hailed a taxi to take us to the Star Ferry terminal. We took the short ride across to Hong Kong Island, where my mother commandeered another taxi.

Our first stop was the local office for my father's company. We took the elevator to the floor where the manager had his office. My mother disappeared into his office while my sister and I waited in the lobby. She was inside for a long time, which gave me an opportunity to walk around and look out of the windows. I didn't understand what was going on and was mostly bored and annoyed. I learned later that she was trying to get us passage aboard a ship bound for either Australia or New Zealand. But the manager was unable to do anything for us because most of the ships already had departed. The rest were booked solid by people trying to escape from Hong Kong.

There was good reason for the anxiety of the people in this British colony. The Japanese Army was already on the border between Hong Kong and Guangdong Province of China, and had been since early in Japan's war against China. At any moment they were about to invade British territory, and then what would happen to all of the people trapped there?

My mother emerged from the manager's office with a discouraged look. Finally, in my tiny brain, I began to realize there was a problem. When adults get worried, their children often pick up on it, and they too start to reflect that worry even though they may not understand the cause. I now became quite agitated, and started asking dozens of questions that my mother was either unable or unwilling to answer. Instead she chose action.

We next went to the British administrative office for the colony. After she gave her name to a clerk at the desk, she rejoined us to sit on a row of hard chairs lined against the wall. The lobby was dim and smoky, and dozens of other people waited patiently for their turn to talk to officialdom. Time dragged slowly. There was really nothing for us to do. On top of that, I was getting hungry, which caused me to get whiney. Somehow my mother coped with all of these problems until finally she was called to go to another office. My sister and I were left to wait in the smoky room, and my sister, with great patience, managed to keep me entertained for the few minutes our mother was gone.

Finally she returned and announced we were going to return to the ship on which we arrived. She could not get any help finding a ship bound for one of the safer British colonies. We would take our chances with the old coal collier. The captain told my mother that as soon as it had been reprovisioned, the ship would sail to the nearest friendly port outside the sphere of Japan's growing domination. This would at least get us away from the impending Japanese invasion of Hong Kong.

My biggest concern was how my father and brother would meet us for Christmas if we were leaving Hong Kong. My mother tried to smooth this over by saying they would be perfectly all right where they were. We would get together just a little later when all of this unpleasantness was over. Although her words were certainly reassuring, I'm sure she did not hold much faith in her own wishful thinking. After all, they were both in cities the Japanese already occupied and had little chance of going anywhere else.

After stopping for a fast lunch, we returned to the Star Ferry and crossed back to Kowloon. As the ferry crossed the straits, we could see an almost empty harbor. Practically all of the ships had departed. It was mid-afternoon by the time we arrived at the collier and were welcomed back aboard, returning to the same stateroom we had on the previous leg of our voyage. My mother was not surprised to see Mrs. Costain still on board. No one was getting out of Hong Kong unless they had prior commitments on a ship.

Late that afternoon, the ship pulled away from the dock and sailed through the empty harbor. The captain told us we were sailing to Manila on the last ship to leave Hong Kong.

The next morning, the Japanese army crossed the border into the British colony and quickly conquered Kowloon and the New Territories. Shortly thereafter, they landed on Hong Kong Island. After a couple of weeks of fierce fighting, the remaining British forces surrendered on Christmas Day, 1941.

British and other Allied civilians were moved to a concentration camp on a remote area of the island, where they were held under uncomfortable conditions until the war ended in August, 1945. Today, busloads of tourists visit that same place, without realizing what it had once been, to bargain for clothes, electronics, and other goods at the sprawling Stanley Marketplace. The surviving British troops were held in even harsher conditions, and many were used as slave labor in building the railroad from Burma to Siam depicted in the movie *Bridge on the River Kwai*. Many soldiers did not survive long enough to see the end of the war.

But we were safely away before all of this happened, as the ship set a course for a safe harbor, Manila. The capital of the Philippines, Manila was surrounded by major American military bases. A large army defended the main island of Luzon, and many people thought the Japanese would never attempt to invade American territory. Again, we would be protected, and I'd be able to observe this exciting, now-expanded, war from a discreet distance.

FIVE

A SAFE HAVEN

After leaving Hong Kong, we slipped back into the comfortable shipboard routine we had developed during our journey from Tientsin. The ocean was warmer and the days comfortable and balmy. This voyage took three and one-half days, and early in the morning of December 12, we approached the entrance to the immense bottle-shaped Manila Bay.

As the sky brightened to the east, the sun peeped over the rim of the Central Cordillera, the mountainous backbone of Luzon Island. I had risen early to see our approach to Manila because members of the crew had told me exciting stories about the beauty of the city and the technical marvels at its docks. It really intrigued me when they said we would not use a gangway from the ship to the dock, but instead there would be a bridge to a building on the dock.

I climbed up to the flying bridge and looked over this peaceful scene as the ship slipped through the channel that separated the jungle covered Bataan Peninsula from the lower-lying fortified island of Corregidor, which marked the entrance to the bay. There was a warm breeze from the motion of the ship, and I was quite comfortable in a light shirt and shorts. I hung onto the railing in awe of this magnificent scenery. A few other ships were also in the bay and proceeding at a measured pace towards the harbor, which was not yet visible at the far end of the bay.

It was going to take time for the ship to sail into Manila at the reduced speed we were making, so I returned to the salon to get breakfast. By that time, my mother, Mrs. Costain, and Lucy had also arrived, so we dined together. The captain sat at a nearby table also having breakfast. As I finished my meal, I looked out the window of the navigation bridge. Taller buildings in Manila were beginning to show in the distance, sparkling in the sunlight. Then something strange happened. Black flowers appeared to bloom above the city.

I turned to the captain, who was sitting nearby happily munching on toast, eggs, and bacon while looking through some papers spread before him, and asked what was happening over the city. He looked up, then uttered a typically British oath, "Bloody hell! It's a Japanese air raid." I'm sure that if my mother had been forewarned, she would have covered my ears, but as it turned out I now had a new expression to add to my collection of little understood French, Italian, Chinese, and American expressions.

But that was merely a fleeting thought because I immediately realized that here was a real war, and I had a front row seat. I made a dash for the stairway up to the flying bridge so I could get a better view, but the captain caught me and held me back. He then explained to his passengers that he wanted us to stay in the middle of the salon, away from the windows. It was dangerous because falling shrapnel from anti-aircraft shells could seriously harm us.

That was a disappointment, but not a disaster. I could still see out of the navigation bridge windows and those on the sides of the salon. The ship was now moving very slowly in the direction of Manila, as were several other ships ahead of us, preparing to enter the port. Life was briefly suspended for those of us floating out in the bay while we waited for the Japanese to do whatever damage they were going to do.

Soon we could see billows of black smoke rising to the southwest of the main part of the city. One of the officers looked at the chart, and then told us that it was coming from Cavite, the large American naval base. This obviously was the main target of the Japanese air raid. So far, he said, it appeared that the attack was against U.S. Navy ships and fixed military installations ashore. There was no indication that the Japanese were hitting civilian shipping.

No sooner had he said this than we heard the sound of an increasing rumble. It was coming from our left, or the port side of the ship, so I looked out of the windows on that side. At first I didn't see anything, then quite clearly I noticed a twin-engine aircraft close to the water coming straight at us. It flew directly over us with a hideous roar and so low that we all instinctively ducked. When it passed, I ran to the starboard side and could see the aircraft banking to turn towards Manila. On its side was painted a big red ball in the middle of a white field. It was a Japanese bomber!

A few hundred yards ahead, another cargo ship, its deck loaded with lumber, also was heading for the port. We could clearly see through the navigation bridge window as the bomber lined up with it fore and aft, then dropped two bombs. One bomb hit the water right alongside the ship, sending up a tremendous geyser of water; the other bomb hit squarely in the middle of the load of lumber.

"Look," I screamed. "That Japanese plane bombed the ship ahead of us!" I'm not sure if the others had seen the bomb falling, but now they rushed to look out the window. I thought I heard Mrs. Costain give a low moan, but my sister and mother just looked stunned. Shortly, smoke started rising from the ship, and we could see flames licking at the wood.

The captain immediately gave a quick series of orders, and the ship slowly started to turn to port and gather speed away from Manila. He came back into the salon to tell us that it was unsafe to continue into Manila harbor since the Japanese were targeting the ships. What about the burning ship? The crew was in no immediate danger. They had reported by radio that the damage was superficial, and they expected to get the fire under control fairly quickly. Then our captain told us that his plan was to seek a safer location farther along the coast and anchor until it was safe to return to the harbor.

∞ ∞ ∞

Now began one of the most pleasant interludes of our journey. The captain found a sheltered cove about half way up the Bataan Peninsula. For the next few days we adopted a comfortable routine of spending the daylight hours on land and then returning to the ship in the evening. The Japanese did not have night bombing capability, but if they came during the day and sank the ship, we would be safely out of the way.

Each dawn after an early breakfast, the passengers and crew would climb down into the two lifeboats and row to the beach at the head of the cove. It was a small beach, probably no more than fifty feet long and about eight feet wide, sloping fairly steeply from the water up to the jungle. There was virtually no surf, and the small waves lapped gently at the coarse sand. The water was pleasantly warm and the air temperature balmy without the oppressive heat that would come later in the year. By any measurement, it was a tropical paradise. I wore only a pair of shorts, and for the first few days had to be cautious about how much time I spent in the direct sun. But after a few days, my skin began to turn a nice protective brown color.

The passengers stayed together near one end of the beach, while the crew dispersed themselves along the rest of the beach. The adults spent the day reading and gossiping, while my sister and I swam a great deal, built sandcastles, and did some reading. We'd have a picnic lunch of sandwiches the cook had made before we left the ship in the morning, then step a few feet into the shady jungle to take a nap. It was not a dense jungle, but fairly open with mostly coconut palms, so it was easy to find a soft flat place to lay out a blanket and doze.

On our second day on the beach, I was sitting on a rotting log at the edge of the jungle eating my sandwich. Suddenly, I felt insects crawling all over my legs, stinging me. I looked down and discovered an army of large red ants crawling on me, occasionally taking bites out of my flesh that burned horribly. Jumping up, I screamed and started flailing at the nasty critters. My mother jumped up, and seeing what was happening also started beating at the crawling ants. The ships crew, hearing the commotion, also gathered around. The ants were too numerous to get rid of, so I finally got the brilliant idea of jumping into the ocean, which not only got rid of the insects, but also soothed the burning from the bites. When I emerged from the water, I now had to face the worst part of my ordeal, which was to hear my friends in the crew laughing and calling out, "Hey, you got ants in your pants?"

By the third day, sitting on the beach was starting to get old, so Mrs. Costain, my mother, sister, and I decided to do some exploring. Walking into the jungle, we discovered a coconut plantation and found a path running parallel to the water. We followed it for a ways and came upon a Filipino village. The villagers were as surprised to see us as we were to see them; but with exquisite courtesy, they invited us to join them for lunch. We were ushered into one of their homes, which was on stilts about eight feet above the ground. Underneath were pens for chickens and pigs. I gingerly walked up the sloping bamboo ramp to the entrance and walked carefully into the one big room.

The house was built entirely of bamboo, palm fronds, and tied together with rattan. Under the floor were large diameter bamboo poles that were the support beams. The floor itself was composed of narrow strips of split bamboo. The walls and roof were also held up with large diameter bamboo. The roof was made of woven palm fronds resembling roof tiles called *nipa*, and the walls were made of braided fronds called *sawali*. It was the typical construction for villages throughout the countryside, and we later learned that the construction techniques were applicable to our own needs.

As I stepped into the room, the bamboo slats of the floor sagged uncomfortably under my feet, so I made it a point to try to step only on the bamboo beams. When the owners noticed, they laughed and told me that the floor was perfectly strong enough to hold my weight. It seemed like I was destined to embarrass myself on numerous occasions during our stay in this province.

One afternoon as we were lounging on the beach, an outrigger canoe filled with Filipino fishermen slid into the cove. They beached nearby and came over to talk with us. This was a real outrigger canoe, quite long, carved from a tree trunk, and with a bamboo outrigger lashed to one side. The fishermen noticed me admiring their craft and invited me to go for a ride. This was a real thrill because, unlike the lifeboats, the sides were just a few inches above the water. In the evening when it was time to return to the ship, the captain invited the fishermen to join us for dinner. I insisted that I wanted to return on the canoe, and everyone indulged my whim, so I had another thrilling ride.

On another day, we walked through the jungle away from the water. A few hundred yards inland, we discovered a dusty dirt road. We walked along it for a little way, and soon heard the sound of the grinding motor of a truck. A cloud of dust blew towards us, and the truck slowed to pass. It was an American Army truck, and the back was filled with soldiers, real soldiers with flat helmets and guns. I was so excited that I jumped up and down and waved. The soldiers started grinning, and waved back, spreading their fingers in the V for victory sign.

The presence of soldiers nearby gave us added confidence that we were in a safe place. Little did I realize until many years later when I visited Bataan and drove along this very same road, now paved and with memorial markers, that this was to become the route of the infamous Bataan Death March. Just a few months after this December day in 1941, 70,000 soldiers, the remains of the American and Filipino armies, would be cruelly marched along this road, thousands dying of thirst, heat, dysentery, and Japanese bullets, bayonets, and swords. Of the Americans on this march, more than 80 percent would be dead before the war ended.

∞ ∞ ∞

During the afternoon of the eighth day of our sojourn on the beach, a Japanese aircraft flew over, following the coast. That evening, the captain told us that it was time that he delivered us to Manila. The Japanese followed a fairly routine bombing schedule, and the captain figured he had just enough time to get in and out of Manila between the morning and the afternoon air raids. Unfortunately, our holiday on a tropical desert island was about to end, all too soon for me, as civilization beckoned.

The next morning, we weighed anchor and started to complete our aborted journey to the port. As we left Bataan, we could see that every cove along the peninsula had a ship anchored in it. What a tasty target it must have been for the Japanese, and we now understood the captain's haste to get away. He did not want to be responsible for his passengers if the ship was sunk and we were stranded in the middle of Bataan.

Shortly before noon, we approached the city, which was covered by a pall of smoke, mostly blowing from Cavite and other military installations. We passed a few ships sunken in the bay, but had no difficulty maneuvering to the dock. I stared fascinated at the hulks, with only their masts and the top of their superstructure showing. I lost any interest on how we would get onto the dock, and didn't care whether it was by bridge or gangway as long as we got there fast.

Immediately after the ship docked, Mrs. Costain, my mother, my sister, and I went down the gangway. Our luggage was brought to us on the dock. Staying only a few minutes, the ship pulled away and departed. It wasn't until several months later that we learned that shortly after our ship returned to the cove, a series of Japanese attacks were launched and all the ships anchored along the coast were sunk, ours among them.

Now that we'd landed in a strange city, we had to find a place to stay. Mrs. Costain said she had friends nearby, and she would call them for assistance. That was the last time I remember seeing her and never learned what happened to her. But it was an unsettled time and place, and not unusual for people to disappear without a trace. Years later, I did find her name in the census of prisoners in the Santo Tomas Internment Camp, so I presume she survived the war.

My mother took immediate control of our situation and flagged a taxi to take us to the Manila office of my father's company. There, the manager gave her a briefing on the situation in Manila and arranged a room for us in the Manila Hotel. Being an important American businessman in this American territory, the manager had been briefed by the High Commissioner, who was the American governor of the Philippine Islands Commonwealth. The outlook for Allied civilians in the city was good, and the High Commissioner was quite positive that the Japanese would never be able to enter the city with General MacArthur commanding an army of over 100,000 American and Filipino troops, with reinforcements surely to soon be sent from America.

The Manila Hotel, a large six-story building, was located adjacent to the waterfront, roughly half way between the docks and the High Commissioner's residence, which was the seat of the American government. It was beautiful and operated in the tradition of the finest Asian hotels, which were among the most luxurious in the world. Years later when I visited Manila, I again stayed at the Manila Hotel and marveled at how this dowager had maintained her beauty and prestige through a very difficult time. It had been expanded and heightened by many floors, but I could still recognize some of the old features that remained. Because of its historical significance, the hotel had an archivist, and on my later visit she guided me around the hotel and to the archives, which had many photos of how it looked in the 1940s. A wave of nostalgia hit me, because I recognized so much from my first visit. Both that old hotel and I had recovered nicely from some very hard times.

The Philippine Islands Commonwealth government was located at the Malacañang Palace a mile or so away from the hotel on the other side of the Pasig River. One side of our hotel overlooked the harbor and the other overlooked the Intramuros, the colorful original Spanish walled city that dated back to the

16th Century and filled the area adjacent to where the Pasig River entered the bay. Just a block away was the main business district, bisected by wide tree-lined avenues. The hotel was ideally located to take advantage of this beautiful city known as "The Pearl of the Orient." General MacArthur knew a good thing when he saw it, because he took up residence for his family in the hotel and made it his military headquarters.

We were now happily ensconced in this impregnable city that American officialdom had declared would be an island of safety in a Japanese-dominated world. Christmas was just four days off, and we could enjoy ourselves until after the holidays, when my mother would have to make another decision about our future. But if we were safe from the effects of war, except for the occasional bombing raid, what about my father and brother? They were both trapped in Japanese occupied cities when the war against America started, and surely they must be in great danger.

Six

My Father's Story

While we were safely ensconced in the Manila Hotel wondering about the safety of the rest of our family, my father was in Tientsin under house arrest by the Japanese Military Police. At the time of the Japanese attack on Pearl Harbor, his first indication that anything was amiss was at dawn of December 8 when the phone rang and a friend from the skeleton crew left at the American Consulate informed him of the attack. They expected the Japanese to enter the Consulate at any moment, so they were frantically destroying sensitive documents. Japanese patrols were setting up roadblocks throughout the city. The Marine barracks, surrounded by a large detachment of heavily armed soldiers, was expected to surrender momentarily. He advised Max to stay in his home until he was notified how the Japanese were going to treat American civilians.

Max was extremely agitated. Elsie and the two children should have arrived in Hong Kong the previous afternoon, and though the Japanese did not occupy the British colony, their troops were on its border and could invade at any time. He called the British Consulate and inquired about his wife and family, to find out if the Foreign Office had any record of their arrival. The Consulate personnel told him that they still had radio contact with the Hong Kong government and would pass on his request for information. However, they did not know how long it would be before the Japanese entered their compound in Tientsin and confiscated their radio gear.

His next call was long distance to his son, John, in Shanghai. When he tried to put the call through, though, the switchboard operator told him that all long-distance circuits had been cut. A short while later, someone from the British Consulate called to report that the Foreign Office in Hong Kong had received no word that his family had arrived in the colony. They could not have known that the typhoon had delayed our voyage, and that our ship did not arrive until that same morning, and it was late in the morning before my mother went to the Foreign Office.

Max now was in a state of frustration. He had no idea where his family was, and he was confined to his home. Being both gregarious and action oriented, he could neither join his friends to commiserate, nor move around the city to pound on doors and get things moving. He was forced to stay in his home and wait for whatever would happen next. The isolation was reinforced when he looked out of the front window and saw Japanese military vehicles patrolling the street. To make matters worse, the phone switchboard was soon closed to all but official Japanese traffic.

He realized that it was just a matter of time before the Japanese rounded up the Americans and other enemy civilians. He thought that they would put them in some central location, like the racetrack, until the Japanese decided how to dispense with them. He decided to hide some of the family valuables, since he expected that his home would soon be searched. He buried them in the dirt floor of the basement storage room, moving various stored household articles over the burial site.

Within the week, a Japanese officer, accompanied by a group of soldiers and a representative of the Swiss Embassy, arrived at the front door. The soldiers searched the house for articles the Japanese considered contraband. When the soldiers completed the search, leaving our home in disarray, the Swiss diplomat recorded what had been taken. He told Max that a receipt would be issued for the confiscated items, including our expensive shortwave radio and our Pontiac.

Max was held as a prisoner of the Japanese Imperial Army and was not to leave his home. If he were ever caught outside, he would be severely punished; but he could keep some of his servants, and they would have to do the marketing and procure any personal items that he needed. His confinement would last until the Japanese decided whether to place the civilians in a concentration camp, like they were doing in Shanghai.

∞ ∞ ∞

For almost a year and a half, my father was held incommunicado. He was frustrated and concerned because he didn't know what had happened to his family. His repeated requests to the Swiss Consulate representative yielded no information. He was able to have Liu Lau, the major domo of his servants, smuggle out and stash the large set of sterling flatware that the family had used for dinner parties in better times, and some other valuables. But time dragged. He was never told about what had happened to my brother John and to us. He had no clue that we had escaped Hong Kong and had safely reached the Philippines.

Then in March 1943, a Japanese officer came to his home and ordered him to pack one small suitcase and to join a group of other civilians. They were taken to the Weihsien Civilian Assembly Center on the Shantung Peninsula. Here, he shared a small room with 11 other men in what had once been a Presbyterian training center. The room was unheated and bitterly cold; but as spring progressed, the weather grew milder and the freezing nights became just a bad memory. In May the Japanese transferred him to Shanghai along with a small group of men, women, and children. He now hoped he would at least be able to find out about John, and may even be moved into the same camp where John was being held.

The train trip to Shanghai was uncomfortable. He joined a mass of people crowded into an old third-class passenger coach with hard benches for seats. The journey took twice as long as normal during peacetime because the train was frequently shunted to sidings to allow more important traffic to pass. The passengers were a strange mixture of families, including women and children, diplomats, businessmen, and missionaries. Max couldn't piece together the rationale for bringing this particular group to the concentration camps.

However, when they arrived in Shanghai, they were not put in a concentration camp; instead, they were loaded on the *Asama Maru,* a Japanese passenger ship. It was then that they learned they were part of a prisoner exchange and were going home to America. But their ordeal was not over. The ship was overcrowded, hot, uncomfortable, with abominable food. The daily meal consisted of a cup of rice full of maggots and weevils.

The *Asama Maru* stopped in other ports to take on additional passengers, and the accommodations became even more confined. After several weeks at sea, the *Asama Maru* arrived at Mormugao in the Portuguese colony of Goa on the west coast of India. After docking, the passengers were herded onto the deck. Nearby was a great white passenger ship flying the Swedish flag, and they could read the name—*S.S. Gripsholm.* They had finally arrived at the exchange point where Japanese prisoners would be brought to the *Asama Maru* and American prisoners would be taken to the *Gripsholm.*

But now there was a delay in the transfer procedure. As they stood on deck in the hot tropical sun waiting, no one could understand what was happening. Then a whispered rumor passed through the assembled throng. One of the Japanese repatriates on the *Gripsholm* decided that he did not want to return to Japan. He had jumped overboard into shark-infested waters and was not recovered. Now there was an imbalance of prisoners since there was one more American to exchange than there was Japanese. That was unacceptable to the Japanese, and they were not going to allow the exchange to proceed until it was in equal numbers.

The impasse continued until finally one of the Americans volunteered to remain on the Japanese ship and return to confinement. That sacrifice broke the logjam, and finally the exchange started. As the Americans progressed down one gangway on the *Asama Maru*, the Japanese climbed another. The same exchange procedure was followed on the *Gripshom*, with the Americans embarking while the Japanese debarked. The difference in released prisoners was graphic as the sleek, healthy, well-fed Japanese passed the starving, disease-ridden Americans staggering along supporting each other.

The Swedish crew on the *Gripshom* was extremely compassionate; and during the next few weeks on the voyage to New York, they made every effort to make their passengers comfortable and to feed them well. By the time the trip ended, the Americans had regained their strength and had greatly improved dispositions.

∞ ∞ ∞

In August 1943, the *Gripsholm* docked in New York, finally bringing the former prisoners home. When they went down the gangway to the dock, officials sorted them out and directed them to various tables in the warehouse that lined the dock. Max sat down across from a friendly official who checked his papers and then asked him a few questions about what he had seen the Japanese doing in China. Although he had been isolated for almost a year and a half, he knew a great deal about the Japanese as a result of his business and his travels in China before the war. The official then told him there would be follow-up interviews to get more detailed information.

Max settled into a New York hotel. Soon, people from the New York office of American International Underwriters, the parent company for which he worked, contacted him. He discovered that he knew a few people because at one time or another they had been assigned to work in China. They were extremely solicitous, entertained him in their homes, and kept him busy while he waited to see what would happen next. He also was interviewed for hours by a number of government agents who were looking for every smidgen of information he had about Japanese activities in China. Despite the official attention, Max still had not learned about the whereabouts of his family. They had been constantly on his mind since they disappeared almost two years earlier.

In the second week after his arrival, Max received a call from a secretary at the office of American International Underwriters who asked if he could meet with Neil Starr, the Chairman of the company. Neil, the founder of the company in China during the 1920s, had previously hired Max to head the company's operations in North China. Max was eager for the meeting with his old friend and mentor. When he arrived at Neil's office, Max was greeted warmly. After reminiscing for a few minutes, Neil told him he had news about Max's family and where they were. Max was both relieved and worried. He now knew they were all alive, but their circumstances weren't the best.

How had Neil obtained this information? Neil explained. After the war started in Europe, President Roosevelt authorized a covert organization to collect intelligence information and prepare for operations behind enemy lines in the event America became involved in the war. The organization's cover name became the Office of Strategic Services or OSS. The President picked William Donovan, a World War I Medal of Honor winner, to head the organization. Neil Starr and "Wild Bill" Donovan became friends when they both served in the trenches in France during World War I.

Because the British were tutoring Donovan's organization, its entire focus had been on preparing for an European war. When Japan attacked Pearl Harbor, he had to scramble to develop a program in Asia. Donovan turned to his old friend Neil Starr, who was known as a "China Hand," to organize it. Neil needed all the help he could get to develop intelligence on the Japanese, and many of the people who could help him were prisoners in Asia. He therefore insisted that people he knew and trusted be put on the prisoner exchange list.

Max was eager to get involved in the war against Japan, which had separated his family and put it in such dire jeopardy. So it was not just in gratitude to Neil that he willing agreed to join the OSS. At 55 years old, Max was not asked to become involved in field operations. Instead, the organization would use his knowledge of China, its culture, his many acquaintances, and his fluency in the Mandarin Chinese language to provide liaison with Chiang Kai Shek and his supreme command. Although serving as a civilian, he would be given the equivalent rank of Colonel, a large promotion from his last rank of 2nd Lieutenant in the U.S. Army in France.

During the next few months, Max was sent to a survival training school and then briefed in detail on his mission. He soon found himself on a ship in a slow-moving convoy bound for India. Arriving on the west coast of India, he was assigned transportation on a supply flight to Assam in the northeast of the country, which was the jumping off point for the supply flights into China over the Himalayas. Those flights, known as "flying the hump", were extremely dangerous, but they were the only access into China, which had been isolated by the Japanese invasion of the coastal regions. First, the overloaded aircraft had to fly through the mountains, not being able to gain enough altitude to fly over them. Then they had to navigate through Japanese airspace before reaching their destinations in south central China. The mortality rate was extremely high, and could only be tolerated as an expedient of all-out warfare.

Max's flight into China was aboard a twin-engine C-47, affectionately known as a "Gooney Bird." The cargo was mainly supplies and ammunition with just a handful of passengers in uncomfortable canvass rack seats. It was bitterly cold as they flew through the Himalayas, and they were happy when they were past the mountains and descended to lower altitude to elude Japanese fighters. But that was when trouble started. One of the engines failed.

The plane was too overloaded to fly with just one engine, so the pilot ordered the passengers to strap on parachutes and jump. My father had been given parachute training in survival school, but this was the first time he had to jump from a real airplane. Fortunately, he landed safely in a paddy field and only had to suffer being wet and smelly. They had already reached Chinese occupied territory, and the survivors were soon picked up by a Chinese patrol and taken to an American airbase. From here, Max caught a flight to his planned destination of Chunking.

∞ ∞ ∞ ∞

Max was responsible for providing liaison between the American command and the Chinese command for the China Theater of operations. He soon became totally frustrated by the lack of progress the Chinese were making in fighting the Japanese. The Americans wanted the Chinese to be more aggressive in attacking the Japanese, but the Chinese always had excuses why they could not. They were not yet fully trained, they didn't have enough equipment, and the Americans were not bringing in supplies fast enough.

The American command knew how many divisions the Chinese had because they were training many of them. Providing materiel was problematic because all of the bombs, ammunition, and other supplies had to be flown across India, then over the Himalayas. But each succeeding month resulted in higher inventories of these supplies. So the Americans knew what the Chinese Army had, and in their judgment it was more than sufficient to sustain an offensive against the Japanese. What the Americans suspected was that Chiang Kai Shek was diverting many of his men and supplies to fight the Communists, who were technically China's allies in fighting the Japanese.

The intrigue and politics involved between the two sides were so complex that it was virtually impossible for Max to do an effective job. A year and a half after he arrived in Chunking, the Chinese had only accomplished a few small offensives against the Japanese. The Americans had given up plans of using the Chinese to clear a path to the East China Sea in order to provide a base for the invasion of Japan.

After the war, my father turned in his resignation to the OSS. He requested that his discharge become effective in China, because he intended to remain in the country where he was born to rebuild his life. But for our family, the consequences of the war were far from over, and my own lovely little war had become increasingly bitter and would continue for yet another two years beyond the Japanese surrender.

SEVEN

MY BROTHER'S STORY

While we were in Manila, we probably didn't need to worry much about my brother, John Dare Lorenzen. Since he went off to college, John had become an independent and self-sufficient young man. His middle name, Dare, I assumed, was adopted from his mother's side of the family. He was very young when she died, and my father was left to raise him alone. When he was still not more than a baby, the Amah took care of him, but as he grew older, my father wanted a stronger male role model for him. He, therefore, enrolled him in a boarding school where John would associate with other boys his own age, while getting an excellent education. He also roamed through the Chinese sections of the city, making many friends, polishing his Chinese language skills, and getting a much different kind of education.

John was nine years old when my father remarried. He was thrilled that he would now have a normal family with a father and mother. But he liked his school, and decided to stay there, except for holidays and the summer vacation. When he was home, he became very attached to his dad's new wife, and enjoyed the fact that she loved sports and was always ready for a new adventure with him and his father.

It wasn't long before my sister was born. Then I came along on the eve of John's 13th birthday. John adored us, and whenever he was home, spoiled us with treats and was always inventing new games to play. We in turn loved him, and we had a happy family life together.

In the spring of 1941, John graduated from his preparatory school, and my father agreed that he should go to Shanghai to start college in the autumn. He was a lanky, good looking, dark-haired boy with blue eyes and a crooked grin, standing more than six feet tall. He was gregarious and had many friends in both the Western and Chinese communities of Tientsin.

When he arrived in Shanghai, he quickly made friends at his college, but was a little chagrined to find that he could not communicate and make friends in the Chinese community there because they spoke a different dialect. He immediately set out to correct that by learning their language. He had a quick mind for language and already understood that giving a word a different sound changed its meaning, so he was soon adept in communicating with the locals.

John shared his father's love of hunting, and had brought the 12-gauge shotgun that his father had given him on his 16th birthday. After he was established at school, he took to hitching a ride, or taking public transportation to the outskirts of the city where he found fields and marshes that were ideal for hunting migratory fowl. He tramped through the countryside on weekends, often stopping in small villages to visit. Since he really had no use for the birds that he bagged, he would give them to the Chinese friends he was making in the villages. They returned his largesse by inviting him to dine with their families and to spend the night. This allowed him to extend the range of his travels further from the city than if he had to return each night.

John took one of his two-day jaunts on the weekend of December 6 and 7, returning to his dormitory at the college on Sunday evening. He was awakened early on Monday morning by the excited buzz of his dormitory mates, who had just received information about the Japanese attack on Pearl Harbor. At noon, the college president called an assembly and told the students, all of whom were Westerners, that he expected the Japanese to round them up and detain them for the duration of the war. In the meantime, they had been ordered by the Japanese garrison to remain inside their residence, and anyone found outside would be severely punished. From the years of Japanese occupation of China, John knew that the term "severe punishment" usually meant beatings, incarceration under starvation conditions, and possibly execution. He decided at that moment that he would not stay around to be incarcerated by a people he detested for what they had done to the Chinese, and was willing to take the risk.

He didn't know how much time he had before it would be too late to get away, but expected that the longer he waited, the more difficult it would be to escape the city undetected. He decided to leave that night. He pondered whether to invite any of his friends to join him, but then decided that his chances were better if he went alone, particularly since none of them were as proficient in Chinese as he. They would find it more difficult to fit into the indigenous population, which would increase their risk of being discovered by the Japanese. He had no doubt about what would happen if the Japanese captured them in the countryside after they had been ordered to remain in their residence.

John put together a bundle of food and clothing to take with him, and decided to leave his beloved shotgun because it would make him too conspicuous on the street late at night. After his dorm mates had settled in for the night, he snuck out and started for the outskirts of the city. He had to stay in the shadows, and duck into a dark place whenever a Japanese patrol went by. He was the only person on the street as the Japanese were enforcing a curfew.

By dawn, he was well away from the city, but he was tired from his long trek. He needed to find a place to sleep so he could carry on his journey the next night. His goal was to arrive at a small village where he had friends and hope that they would be willing to hide him through the daylight hours. He knew that he was putting their lives at jeopardy because if the Japanese searched the village and found him, they would all be executed.

On the other hand, the villagers hated the Japanese so much that they might be willing to take the risk.

His friends didn't hesitate to hide him. They were also innovative. Knowing that he was too large to fit into the peasant clothing they could provide him, one of the women stitched together a replica in a size that would fit him. When he awoke at dusk, they presented him with the dark pants, jacket, and cotton shoes that were their own typical dress. He realized that he could never pass as a Chinese with his large stature and blue eyes, but from a distance, if he stooped, he might get away without identification. They also told him that there was a guerilla band about a day's walk distance, and they provided him with a guide to find them.

∞ ∞ ∞

When the Japanese declared war on China in 1937, the Koumintang government had for years been fighting to exterminate the Communists. But with a common enemy, they suspended their enmity and agreed to cooperate in fighting the Japanese. So the Kuomintang, headed by Chiang Kai Shek, would use its forces to fight a conventional war, while the Communists under Mao Tse Tung, would fight an unconventional guerilla war. Guerilla bands had been operating in the north and east of China for years now, harassing the Japanese forces. It was one of these bands that John hoped would be able to help him.

The guide led John on hidden pathways, avoiding roads and villages, throughout the night. Just before dawn, they arrived in a remote village, where, the guide told him, someone would contact the guerillas for him. That evening, a small band of armed peasants entered the village, and John was brought out for their inspection. The leader queried him, and was satisfied with answers in rapid-fire dialect of Chinese that he could understand. He agreed to take John into his band and to help him progress westward until he could pass through the Japanese lines into free China.

John was not going to get a free ride though. He was given an old bolt-action rifle and the guerillas studied him carefully as he field stripped, and then reassembled it. During the time the American 15th Infantry had been stationed in Tientsin, they had an annual competition between units, called the "Can Do" competition. Because of his father's involvement with the Army, he was always invited to attend some of the functions, and when John was old enough, he too went to the competition. The soldiers delighted in the youth, and showed him how to shoot a Springfield rifle, then how to maintain it. The rifle the guerillas gave him was not all that different from the Springfield, so John had no problem familiarizing himself with its operation.

For the next few days, John traveled with the guerilla band, which was very mobile and never spent more than a night in a single place. On two occasions, they ambushed Japanese convoys, carrying away supplies, arms, and ammunition. When the band reached the western extremity of its range, the leader transferred him to another guerilla band. Again he was initially treated with suspicion, but quickly gained the band's confidence and was allowed to participate in its operations.

Over the period of several months, John was passed from one guerilla band to the next, mostly moving in a westward direction. One day, the leader of his latest band told him that they were near the front line between the Japanese and Chinese armies. That night, they would escort him through the lines into free China.

Though John expected a more defined fortified demarcation, their travel that night was much like any other. They took hidden paths and avoided a few isolated Japanese patrols until, at dawn, the guerilla leader told him they were now in territory controlled by the Koumintang. Since they were Communists, they did not want a confrontation with the regular Chinese Army troops, so they gave him guidance on how to find one of their units and left him to make his own way. He was in unfamiliar territory and unsure of what kind of reception he would get, but he had come this far, essentially meeting his goal, and he wasn't going to turn back now.

∞ ∞ ∞

In the gathering light, John walked down the narrow trail until it intersected with a dirt road, where he turned in the direction he had been instructed. An hour later, he stumbled into a Chinese infantry patrol. The soldiers immediately surrounded him, pointing their rifles at him, and shouting orders and questions at him. He quickly raised his arms and indicated that he surrendered.

The soldiers bound his arms behind his back and marched him along until they came to a small encampment outside a village. Here he was turned over to an officer for interrogation. John told him of his quest to reach free China, and that his main interest now was to find other Americans and to join them in fighting the Japanese.

The officer's face lit up, and he told John that there was an American Volunteer Group air base only a few miles away. He would arrange to transport John there, and he could make arrangements with them. He told John that they were very happy to have the Americans nearby because the Japanese aircraft were constantly bombing and strafing them, but the Americans were very successful at driving them away. John had read in the news about the Chinese Army's use of American volunteers, and it was just the type of unit that he intended to join.

When the Sino-Japanese war broke out in 1937, the Chinese had only a few antiquated aircraft against a huge modern fleet of Japanese fighters and bombers. The Chinese asked America for help in providing aircraft and pilots to modernize their air force, and President Roosevelt authorized an inactive Army Air Corps Captain name Claire Chennault to recruit volunteers to go to China, along with aircraft that the American Air Force no longer needed. Then, in 1941, the President authorized the shipment of modern P-40 fighter aircraft to China. Armed with these new aircraft, with shark-like teeth painted on the engine cowling, the

Americans started to have devastating effects on the Japanese. The American Volunteer Group came to be known as the Flying Tigers.

Now John was going to have a first-hand opportunity to see this legendary unit. After bumping along for several hours in the back of a Chinese Army truck, they arrived at the airfield. The first thing he noticed was that it was organized in excellent military order, with security guards posted all around it. The second thing he noticed was a handful of vicious-looking P-40s, painted with their characteristic shark teeth, and emblazoned on their fuselage and wings with the Chinese Nationalist flag symbol. Last, he noticed gangs of coolies working on filling bomb craters around the runway.

When he dismounted from the truck, he was taken to a guard shack where an astounded American greeted him. John briefly told his story, and asked if he could join the American Volunteers in fighting the Japanese. The American ignored the last request and immediately took him to the base G2 office. Again he repeated his story to an assembled group of intelligence officers. They started firing questions at him about the route he had taken from Shanghai and the disposition of any Japanese units and bases along the way. He gave them a comprehensive report on what he knew, based on what he had seen or had been briefed by the guerillas.

They let him rest for a couple of days, and have some good American chow, then the commanding officer asked him to his office. He was told that they had checked out his story, which was unusually complete, and would be delighted to have him join their unit. He would be assigned to G2 as a junior member of the intelligence unit.

His job was to gather information from Chinese sources and help to cross-reference this with intelligence from other sources. He started to fly as an observer in a light aircraft used to detect Japanese movements and compared this information with the other intelligence. He was happy with his assignment, and soon learned the fastest way to get into a slit trench when the Japanese bombed their airbase, which was quite often. They had developed an effective bamboo radio, and usually had plenty of time for the pilots to get their P-40s into the air before the Japanese aircraft were overhead. Then they devastated the Japanese bomber formations and their escort of Zeros—the heavier, better armored American aircraft trouncing the more maneuverable Japanese fighters.

During the spring of 1942, President Roosevelt declared that the American Volunteer Group would be incorporated into the American military forces. The new fighter wing became the 23rd Fighter Group, attached to the 14th Air Force, which operated throughout China. John now found himself inducted into the American Army, and was given the rank of Technical Sergeant. Little else changed since the founders of the Flying Tigers were American military personnel and had organized and maintained discipline similar to the Army Air Corps.

In his intelligence work, John and the pilot of the light aircraft would fly past the Japanese lines and compare the information smuggled out by Chinese spies with what they could observe on the ground. It was hazardous work, as the Japanese fighters would be looking for them to shoot them down. On one occasion, a Zero spotted them flying low to the ground and dived towards the small plane, firing its machine guns. The pilot of the light aircraft dodged and maneuvered close to the ground, around trees and hills to dodge the aggressive fighter, at the same time making a radio call to the American base asking for assistance.

A direct hit by the Japanese fighter would have ripped the small plane apart, but the pilot's skill made them a difficult target to hit. Still, some of the machine gun bullets penetrated their engine, and they lost power. They were too low to bail out and the pilot had no choice but to put the aircraft down in a nearby paddy. It was a rough landing and the plane broke apart, but John and the pilot escaped, only to now have to dodge a strafing run by the Japanese pilot.

They scrambled behind a dyke and ducked their heads, virtually into the muck of the field, as the bullets struck around them. The fighter climbed and circled for another attack, and the two men took little comfort from the scant protection of the dyke. But at that moment, they saw the welcome sight of the gleaming shark jaw on a P-40 as it jumped on the attacking fighter. The Japanese pilot made the mistake of concentrating too much on his quarry on the ground and had failed to notice the Flying Tiger coming in low and fast. For that he paid with his life as the machine guns on the P-40 ripped his plane to shreds.

John and the pilot hid out until dark, then were able to find their way back through the Japanese lines. In the morning, they were safely at their base with a good story to tell. But the nonchalant pilots, who faced danger every day against an enemy that vastly outnumbered them, didn't let their close escape go to their heads. Though they won bronze stars for the action, they gained the reputation of being the guys who escaped the Japanese by hiding in a field of crap. At the ripe old age of 20, John was a decorated veteran, had been a guerilla fighter with the most dangerous partisans in Asia, and was now an initiate into the fraternity of some of the toughest fighters in the world.

Many years later, I visited John for a weekend when he was a civilian working for a vague government agency as an instructor at Camp Perry in Virginia. One evening, he threw a party with his fellow "China Hands," who I presume were training a new crop of spooks for the jungles of Viet Nam. During the drunken debauch, his friends again ribbed him about his experience being shit-face in a paddy field with a Japanese taking aim at his raised butt, which demonstrates not just the camaraderie of this elite group, but just how hard it is to lose a reputation once you've gained it.

∞ ∞ ∞

For the next two years, John continued with his work at the remote base in China. But since the unit had become part of the 14th Air Force, its primitive situation improved as more aircraft and pilots were assigned to the base. No longer vastly outnumbered, the air war became more equal, and the pilots' missions started to include escorting American bombers to hit important Japanese positions throughout the eastern part of China.

In late 1943, John received a letter from our father and was relieved to hear that he was safe and back in America. The news about my mother, sister, and I was less comforting, for though our father knew where we were, he didn't know what our conditions were.

During his time with the guerillas, the sanitary conditions were bad, and John had developed a severe case of peritonitis. Our father had developed the same problem in France during World War I, and the result of his affliction was that all of his teeth were removed and he had to deal with false teeth for the rest of his life. John suffered with the condition without complaining, though several teeth were getting loose and he had difficulty chewing. The doctors at his base could do little because they were not trained in oral surgery. On several occasions, they suggested that he be invalided back to the U.S. John refused to go. China was his home and he would stay there until the Japanese were defeated.

Early in 1945, John had been with his unit in the hinterland of China for 3 years. The head doctor became so concerned about his condition that he spoke to the commander of his unit, who immediately cut orders for John to be sent to a hospital in America. He soon found himself on the long trip by plane and ship to a country that he'd never seen. The one compensation was that he was routed through Chunking, and was able to spend a couple of days with our father. Though I wasn't there to observe, I imagine that a lot of booze was consumed in the process of their reunion.

John was admitted to Walter Reed Hospital in Washington D.C., where they started the slow process of rebuilding his gums and health of his teeth and mouth. He soon became an outpatient and was assigned to work in one of the military intelligence units scattered throughout the area. His initial discomfort at the idea of living in America quickly dissipated. He was a tall, good looking, 22-year-old soldier in uniform with an excellent war record, living in a city that abounded with women who had been attracted to the Capitol by the immense number of war-time jobs. Young women outnumbered men by a large margin. How could he possibly go wrong?

But his assignment back in America was also a tremendous benefit to my mother, sister, and particularly to me. The next two times that I saw him were both when he was welcoming me to the shores of America on two different occasions, and without his presence, it would have been a much more difficult time for my family.

EIGHT

A FOOL'S PARADISE

Our stay in the Manila Hotel was a relaxed and happy time for me. My mother, sister, and I had no obligations, and we explored the city within walking distance of the hotel. The Intramuros, with its narrow winding streets and Spanish Colonial architecture, was fascinating to see, not because I understood architecture, but because it was so different from anything I'd seen before. There were interesting alleys, and most important, little stalls where we could buy Filipino delicacies for our lunch and sweets for our afternoon snack. It was here on the afternoon of one of our excursions that I was introduced to that uniquely American commodity—chocolate milk.

The wide avenues of the business district also offered opportunities for exploration. Traffic was very light and crowds were almost non-existent. I think it must have been apprehension about the Japanese landings at Lingayen to the north of Manila and the bombing raids that kept people off the streets, but these things were not obvious to me at the time. Now, when I think back to those days, it must have been delightful, because my recent visits to Manila have shown nothing but gridlocked traffic and a sea of pedestrians.

Christmas came and went with little more than an unexpected Japanese air raid late on Christmas night. When the alarm sounded, we all trooped down the stairs to the hotel basement and huddled there until a short time later, when the all-clear signal sounded. My mother arranged a little Christmas celebration for us in our room by putting up a small scraggly tree of some unknown variety and decorating it with colored paper chains. There were a few gifts under it for both my sister and me, nothing fancy, but enough to get us in the right spirits.

My sister, of course, did not believe in Santa Claus, but she didn't spoil it for me. That was the last year that I had any belief in the jolly elf. Sadly, just a few weeks later, I lost all faith in the magic of the season.

∞ ∞ ∞

We were living in a fools' paradise. The reality of the situation wasn't as apparent to me as a boy as it became in later years. I really didn't know back then that in the months preceding Pearl Harbor, the American administration was telling everyone in Manila to have faith in its ability to defend the Philippines. Meanwhile, diplomats were either surreptitiously leaving the islands or sending their families home to America. There were numerous cases where American residents had made arrangements to leave, but had changed their minds in the face of the earnest pleadings of government officials. In one case, a family of four held reservations for early December on the Pan American Clipper flight to America, only to cancel them at the insistence of the High Commissioner, who assured them that there was absolutely no need to leave the safety of Manila. The government was desperate to avoid having the American populous panic and start a mass exodus from the Philippines. They simply lied about the true situation.

Many years later, American residents who survived the war sued the American government for deceiving them about the true situation in the Philippines. However, the government blocked the lawsuits and denied that the deception was deliberate. To this day, those survivors are still bitter at what the American High Commissioner had done to them.

Yes, MacArthur had an army of over 100,000 men on Luzon, 70,000 of them Filipino Scouts, many of whom he'd brought from other islands to man the defense of the capital. But the truth was that the American troops were ill-equipped, many of them using surplus equipment left over from World War I, and carrying 30-year-old bolt-action Springfield rifles. Not only were the Filipino troops ill-equipped, they also suffered from lack of training and, in some cases, lacked shoes.

MacArthur put together a strategy, called "Plan Orange," for defending the Philippines against Japan. In May 1941, he updated it when President Roosevelt told him that it was his duty to hold the Philippines for as long as possible without help from America, which would be unable to send reinforcements or supplies if the Japanese attacked. MacArthur's plan was to concentrate all of his troops on Bataan and Corregidor and to fight a holding action for as long as he could.

What MacArthur and his successor did with their ill-equipped troops may qualify as a miracle of almost the magnitude of Dunkirk. Although the Army was unable to save these troops from oblivion, they put up such a staunch fight that they completely destroyed the Japanese schedule for over-running the Pacific. They were not able to save the Philippines, but they did save Australia by sapping the strength and will of the Imperial Japanese Army to take on the planned invasion of that country, leaving the Allies with an important outpost in the South Pacific.

∞ ∞ ∞

During the week after Christmas, I began to realize that there was more to the Japanese bombing raids than just to harass us and to spoil my fun. My mother had registered our presence and accommodations with the British Embassy when we first arrived. Now a message came from the Embassy that there was to be a meeting of British citizens to discuss the situation in Manila.

We arrived at the embassy in midmorning. It was a beautiful setting, a large white house surrounded by extensive lush tropical gardens enclosed within a walled compound. While my mother went into the house to attend the meeting, she turned my sister and me loose in the gardens to play with the other children. There were about two dozen of us, and though we had never met before, we were soon actively involved in a number of different games. The gardens and lawns were ideal to play hide and seek, tag, kick ball, and that sort of game. I shudder to think of the damage we must have done to the careful work of an army of Filipino gardeners, but we plowed through flowers and bushes and created divots in the manicured lawns. I'm not sure the embassy had ever had to put up with such uncontrolled mayhem. But as it turned out, it probably didn't really matter in the larger picture of events that were yet to happen.

As we played on a lawn, two Japanese Zero fighter aircraft flew very low over us, pursued by an American P-40. When it was almost directly overhead, the American fighter started firing its machine guns at the Japanese. We all started to run towards a nearby garden house, some of the children screaming. When we got to the shelter, one of the older boys ordered us to get under the tables. He explained that some of the bullets may fall and the table would protect us. The magic of the season was indeed falling away.

Aside from that first momentary panic, we were all surprisingly calm. Seeing one American pursuing two Japanese was an affirmation that our side was superior despite the frequent bombings we heard and the sinking of ships that we saw.

The story my mother was hearing inside the embassy was anything but assuring. It was only later that I surmised what the Ambassador had told the assembled British citizens. General MacArthur had pulled all of his troops out of Manila, leaving it completely undefended. The Philippine government had declared it an "open city," meaning the Japanese could enter it without any resistance. This would be safer for us and would preserve the beauty of Manila from being damaged by fighting.

Furthermore, it was expected that the Japanese would confine all enemy alien civilians, which included the British, in internment camps until hostilities ended. What he meant by the end of hostilities was unclear, because it could mean the time when the Japanese had cleared the American forces from the Philippines, or it could mean the end of the war. A committee of American businessmen had already anticipated this eventuality, and had stockpiled food and medical supplies to support the confined civilian population. They had also chosen several alternative sites for the concentration of civilians, which they would present to the Japanese commander when his troops entered the city.

The Japanese were expected to enter the city within a week. In the meantime, people should stay in their place of residence. When they arrived, the embassy would turn over a list of British citizens to the Japanese commander. It could then be expected that the Japanese would round us up and take us to the concentration facility it had chosen. It would all be done in a very decent and organized manner, or so he hoped.

∞ ∞ ∞

For the next couple of days, we stayed very close to the hotel. My mother figured we needed the exercise, but if the Japanese arrived unexpectedly, she wanted to be close to our base of operations. Since there were very few guests in the hotel, I could extend my playtime by racing around in the lobby and sliding on the polished marble floors without being admonished every few minutes. In fact, the staff and the guests seemed very subdued, and there were seldom more than a small handful of people in the public areas. My physical play world was decreasing in size from the streets of the city to a hotel lobby. Little did I know that soon the boundary would become even more restricted.

New Year's eve was very quiet. There was no large gathering and party at the hotel, with balloons and noisemakers, as we might have expected. Guests dined quietly in the dining room, and outsiders did not join them for music and dancing. The New Year of 1942 was not rung in with any kind of celebration, and we had already gone to bed well before the midnight hour, and more magic of the season slipped away.

New Year's Day, we stayed in the hotel, and I was confined to cavorting around the lobby and the grounds. That evening, my mother took us to the hotel's most formal dining room. We had a feast of succulent pork as only the Filipinos could cook it, and ice cream for dessert. At home, we had always had a feast on New Year's Day. It was almost as big a celebration as Christmas for us. It must have been my mother's Scottish heritage, where Hogmanay was the biggest celebration of the year, with feasts, fun, treats, and visits from friends and family. But this year, perhaps she treated us to the fancy dinner because she expected that it might be the last one for a long time.

On the next day, I was again confined to the hotel grounds. After we arose, we took the elevator to the lobby and went into the restaurant where breakfast was served. We ordered the typical English breakfast that we always had at home—eggs, bacon, and toast, with tea for my mother and milk for my sister and me. Why do I remember such mundane events? It is no doubt because in the succeeding years food became an obsession, and we were inclined to look back at some of our most memorable meals.

Later in the morning, I was playing around in the lobby, when I looked into the dining room where we had eaten earlier. To my surprise, I saw a maid skating around on the marble floors. She had tied coconut husks to her feet, and was dancing and boogying, while quietly singing to herself. I stepped into the room, and when she noticed me, gave a brilliant smile. I looked quizzical, so she explained that this is how she polished the marble floors. It dawned on me how easily she moved, and I made a mental note to ask for some coconut husks so I too could glide across the floors, since my leather-soled shoes didn't work nearly as well.

Returning to the lobby late in the afternoon, I tried a few practice slides, and as I passed a group of businessmen sitting together, one of them raised his hand slightly silencing the others. Then he said quietly, "They're here." I stopped and listened, just as the men did, then heard a quiet rumbling sound that would have been indiscernible over the chatter of voices.

Not waiting for the elevator, I raced up the stairs to our fourth-floor roomwhere my mother and sister were sitting. Like Paul Revere, I burst into the room, panting from the dash, and shouted, "The Japanese are here, the Japanese are here!" We all crowded to the window, and on the main street below, we could see Japanese soldiers marching, soldiers on bicycles and in trucks, and tanks. Japan was taking possession of the capital of the Philippine Islands. A few Filipinos stood on the sidewalk watching, but there was no cheering or celebration.

The Japanese considered themselves liberators of the Philippines, but the vast majority of the Filipinos thought of them as hated invaders. Their lack of enthusiasm in welcoming their liberators, or for inclusion in Japan's Greater East Asian Prosperity Sphere, later would have dire consequences for the Filipino people.

However, the fact that the Japanese now occupied Manila did not upset me. I had lived in occupied Tientsin for most of my life, and knew that the soldiers would not harm us and, in fact, could be quite friendly. I hadn't yet made the connection that the peacetime relationship between the Japanese and we Westerners no longer existed. In wartime, the Japanese had a completely different objective in their treatment of the people they called "enemy aliens," and our lives were about to take a very different direction.

NINE

NOT A COUNTRY CLUB

On the afternoon of January 2, 1942, the Japanese Imperial Army entered Manila. We had to wait another two days to find out what would happen to us, two days of frustrating boredom. Now my mother wouldn't even let me outside the hotel into the surrounding gardens. Japanese soldiers stood outside the hotel doors, and there was no other option for a hyperactive boy than to play inside. I still hadn't located any coconut husks to use as skates.

Then my mother received a phone call from the British Embassy notifying us that we were to board a bus that would be at our hotel the next morning. We would be taken to a place where the Japanese had chosen to assemble all of the enemy alien civilians. On the morning of January 5, we again packed our suitcases and waited in the lobby with the other guests.

Just when I was about to drive my mother crazy, the bus arrived. We were herded between rows of guards onto the bus, each carrying our own suitcase, which we stuffed into the overhead racks. Finally, two armed Japanese guards boarded, standing in the front looking down the rows of seats. The Filipino driver started the engine, let out the clutch, and put the bus into motion towards our unknown destination.

It took only a few minutes to arrive at our destination. We had gone less than two miles, crossing the Pasig River and heading northeast. From the wide main street called Calle España, the bus turned through an arched iron gate in a high iron fence and drove down a long tree-shaded driveway to a wide plaza. Facing the plaza was an ornate three-story concrete building with a tower in the center topped by a cross. On the roof we could see what appeared to be another low building forming a fourth floor.

The plaza was huge. Arranged in the middle of it were a number of tables pushed end-to-end. Several small groups of Japanese soldiers were standing around the periphery with their rifle butts resting on the pavement and bayonets sticking high above their heads—little men with long rifles, as my mother called them. As we got off the bus, we were directed to the tables where a number of American men and women were seated in the sun. It was the registration area for those of us being brought to the plaza in buses and trucks. Our names were on the list provided by the British Embassy, and we were duly entered into the census, assigned a dormitory, and given meal tickets that were good for two meals a day. When my mother asked how long we would be here, no one had an answer.

Following directions, we entered the large building, moving through several hallways until we found our dormitory. It was on the first floor near a far corner of the building from the main entrance where we had entered. Previously, it had been a class-room. Now rows of canvas camp cots were lined up with narrow aisles between them. As instructed, we chose three of the cots that were together and put our suitcases on them as our claim.

We then set out to explore our new environment. Outside the rear door of this large building was another low building, in front of which was a large grassy area with large trees and picnic tables. We decided to spend the rest of the day here, under the trees sheltered from the hot sun. My mother had brought some snacks, and these served as our lunch since no food would be provided for a noon meal. Soon other people began to arrive in our sanctuary, and we found out a little more about this place— the University of Santo Tomas.

∞ ∞ ∞

The Main Building on the University of Santo Tomas campus was a tranquil place in 1941 until the Japanese filled it with civilian prisoners rounded up in Manila and throughout the Philippines. (Photo taken by the author in 2005.)

The University of Santo Tomas, the oldest university in the Pacific, was founded in the Intramuros in 1611 by the Dominican Fathers and was invested with the power to confer degrees by Pope Paul V. In 1927, the University moved to this spacious 65-acre campus in north Manila, a little over a mile away from its original location in the Intramuros. Since its founding, it had been operating continuously until classes were suspended just a month ago at the outbreak of war with Japan.

Fifty years later, I returned to visit the university and marveled at how much the entire campus had changed, while at the same time, how familiar other parts remained. New buildings covered the wide-open spaces that existed in 1942, and the well-regarded university had an enrollment of over 30,000 students. But the Main Building was much as I remembered it, and I could point to the exact spot where various events had happened. The dormitories were returned to classrooms and laboratories, but when I looked inside an empty one, I could immediately visualize how it had looked when it was living space for a crowd of people. However, when I talked with students and faculty, they knew so little of what had happened here and were amazed to learn about the dire and tragic events that marred their prosaic educational institution.

On that first afternoon after our arrival, I set out to explore this vast complex. It took me several days of rambling to thoroughly orient myself within the entire campus, but, by that time, I had a pretty good idea of the layout. Standing on the edge of the plaza where we had arrived, I was facing north. Before me stood the Main Building, where our dormitory was located. To the right was the Education Building, another rather plain concrete three-story structure. To the left, or west, was an enclosed complex—the Seminary—that was out of bounds to us. And far to the left across a grassy playing field, and in front of the Seminary, was the Gymnasium.

On the far side, or north of the Main Building, stood the Annex, a light one-story building with sides and roof made of corrugated galvanized iron. It was quite long and had two full-length bays and one half-length bay separated by courtyards. To the right of it was the large grassy area we had discovered on our first day and where we camped out under the trees during the daytime. Facing the Annex across the grassy area was the Infirmary, another light one-story building, which, in turn, was behind the Education Building.

There were also two extensive playing fields. One filled the southwest corner of the campus in front of the gymnasium; the other filled the southeast corner. Between these two fields were two driveways separated by a grove of trees that extended from Calle España to the plaza. But what most interested me was an area of swampy land with small ponds and streams that was located between the infirmary and the east wall. I was fascinated with water, and the potential for a muddy playground held endless possibilities.

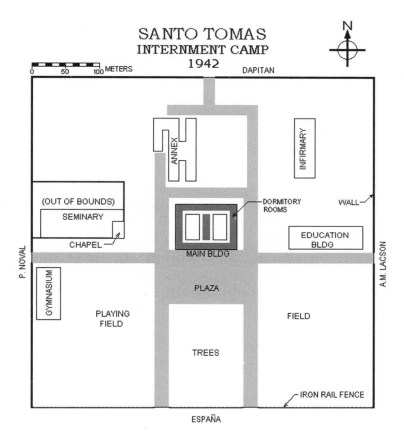

Drawing courtesy of the author.

A 10-foot wall enclosed three sides of the campus. The front of the campus, separated from the plaza by a grove of trees, had an 8-foot-high iron fence through which two arched gated entries provided access to driveways from Calle España to the plaza. The entire campus was roughly square and about one third of a mile on each side. It was ideal for confinement of a large number of civilian prisoners. These five buildings, excluding the seminary, were destined to be our home for as long as the Japanese chose to keep us confined. We were totally at their mercy for our uncertain future.

∞ ∞ ∞

Starting on January 4, 1942, Santo Tomas opened as an internment camp. We were among the first to arrive, which gave us the advantage of getting the better accommodations, if you consider living in a closely packed dormitory with other families as being better. But it was conveniently located to both the public bathrooms and to the cafeteria where we would eat. Later arrivals were packed into even worse conditions. Every day, more people arrived, and the camp population soon reached more than 3,000 in a place never intended as a living facility.

Those first few days were very strange because we were just a mass of people herded together without any seeming purpose. The Americans who started to arrive in large batches told us that the Japanese had advised them to bring clothing and food for three days. They had every expectation that they would soon be returning to their homes. In the interim, they just sat around, gossiped, read, and played cards. When walking around the campus, I'd see large groups of people relaxing on lawns, deck chairs, and picnic benches as if they'd all gathered for a stupendous Fourth of July celebration.

We were fortunate to have meal tickets for the cafeteria in the Annex, which was quite close to our dormitory. Our first meal was on the afternoon of the day we arrived. At 5:00, a line started forming outside of the cafeteria. I was hungry, so I urged my mother and sister to hurry and get in line. After about 15 minutes, we entered the cafeteria and walked along the serving counter, where we were handed a plate with a mess of glop on it.

We sat down at an available table and looked at the unappetizing mess, which was boiled white noodles with canned prunes and sweet brown juice poured on top. I asked my mother what it was, and she told me it was called noodles and prunes. Noodles and prunes! I was never so insulted in my life! How could they serve us such a horrible combination? I liked noodles, and I liked prunes, but how could anyone possibly dream of combining them? It must be some absurd American delicacy.

I was hungry, so I ate what was served, and should have considered myself lucky. There was an inadequate food supply on hand and not nearly enough kitchen space to serve the number of people who were arriving. In those first days, many people had to rely on what they had brought with them, or to buy food from Filipino vendors who lined the fence along Calle España and could pass food or packages through the iron fence bars to those inside the internment camp. Since we were only getting two meals a day, we would walk to the fence and buy something for our lunch from one of the Filipino vendors. This was probably the best meal of the day because it was fresh, and we soon got tired of the corn meal mush with diluted canned milk that we got for breakfast. Our evening meals were more varied, but equally bland, and fortunately we weren't served noodles and prunes again.

After a few days, my mother started to ask me each evening how many times I had been to the bathroom. The new diet had upset my bowels, and I had the trots, soon finding every bathroom available on the campus. When I answered her honestly, she seemed to get rather upset, and would hold her hand to my forehead to see if I had a fever. What I didn't understand was that the crowded conditions, inadequate sanitary facilities, limited kitchen capacity for thoroughly cooking food, and chancy food from through the fence had created an epidemic of dysentery. For most people, dysentery is a discomfort and a cause of dehydration, which itself can become serious. But for small children and other vulnerable people, dysentery can be fatal. Whether I had dysentery, or it was just a reaction to the prunes, I'm not sure, but the problem of loose bowels continued for some time and reoccurred regularly for several months.

One time, I found a bathroom in a remote corner of the campus, and after I was finished, discovered that the toilet would not flush. That was nothing to me, so I exited the stall, where a woman was waiting for her turn. She entered the stall, and then quickly exited as I was leaving the bathroom. She shouted at me, "You tell your mother you have loose bowels!" What is this hang-up that adults have with my natural processes? I wondered. I of course didn't tell my mother since I didn't see any need to further worry her. As it turned out, the epidemic eventually wore itself out as we adapted to the bacteria that caused it, only to be replaced later with much more serious diseases.

∞ ∞ ∞

We continued to camp at the picnic table under the trees that we had found on our first day. But space was limited, and newcomers had to look for their own space. Soon, the grassy field was filled with the desks that had been taken from the classrooms when they were converted into dormitories. These became the bases for many families, who would use them to store their food and sundries under the lift-up top of the desks and as a meeting place for meals.

During the day, I would range throughout the campus, continually finding new wonders, and then return to our meeting place at the picnic table. One day I discovered that the end of the short bay of the Annex was a holding pen for monkeys. These were no doubt laboratory animals for the now defunct university and had little use to the current inmates of the campus. But they were exceptionally fascinating to me as I could approach right to the bars of the cage and watch their antics. One day, I had picked some grass seed-heads, and was idly standing next to the bars tossing them one by one at the monkeys, hoping to get them to stick in their fur.

Suddenly, a monkey reached through the bars and grabbed my hair. Luckily, I pulled away before it could do any more damage than just give me a painful tug. With hair still intact, I decided not to tell anyone about the incident. The next day, my mother asked if I had been playing around the monkeys, and I admitted that I had. She then warned me to stay away from the cage because just that morning a monkey had grabbed a boy's hair and pulled out a large hank, almost scalping him. From that time forward, I stayed away from the monkey cage, and if there was a life lesson in the incident, it was to never trust monkeys, animal or human.

As more children arrived in the camp, we formed groups who would play together and look for mischief. Somehow I hooked up with an American boy somewhat older than me, and it was because of him that I learned the meaning of guilt. One afternoon, he told me that his family had one of the desks on the grassy area, and inside was a jar of jam that his parents said he could have. He urged me to go over to the desk when no one was nearby, then to open the lid and get the jam, which I did. Then we went off to a secret corner and polished off all of the jam in the jar. What a wonderful sweet treat!

Later when I returned to our own camp at the picnic table, my mother's first question was what the red smear on my cheek was. I quickly wiped it off and said, "Nothing." She didn't press the issue, but then I noticed a different family was grouped around the desk where I had taken the jam. It was at that moment I realized that I had stolen the jar of jam. That evening was balmy and pleasant, and a full gibbous moon rose at sunset. It looked to me as if a large yellow face was peering down from the sky, accusing me of such a heinous deed. The guilt just overwhelmed me, and it had such an impressionable affect on my young conscience that I never again felt any urge to take something from another person. It was also a life lesson that I couldn't always trust what a supposed friend was telling me to do.

During that same period, I received another life lesson. When I was exploring the campus, I discovered a large mango tree behind the Annex. Climbing up into the tree, I parted the leaves and discovered a large mango hidden away. It wasn't quite ripe, so I didn't pick it, but rearranged the leaves around it so the mango couldn't be seen from the ground. A few days later, I returned, expecting the mango to now be ripe. During our stay in the Manila Hotel, I had become rapturous over the taste of mangoes. The Philippines are reputed to have the best mangoes in the world—very sweet and with no fibrous pulp around the seed.

I climbed up into the tree and parted the leaves around the hidden mango, and to my extreme disappointment, discovered it was not there. Someone else had discovered my anticipated treat and picked it, even though it was still green. The lesson I learned was that it is better to have a green mango than to have no mango at all. And throughout life, if an opportunity arose, I took it rather than wait to see if something better would come along later. How many times have I missed a great opportunity because I had taken a minor one? I'll never know, but this philosophy has never led to any disappointments.

But the disappointment of losing that mango was soon forgotten as the tempo of life on the Santo Tomas campus changed. No longer were we hopeful that our temporary confinement would soon be over. It became abundantly clear that what was now being called the Santo Tomas Internment Camp was to be our home for a long long time. It was time to start organizing ourselves to adapt to a life as prisoners of the great Japanese imperialistic movement. When would it end? No one had any idea how long we would be confined here, or how difficult life would become.

TEN

SETTLING IN FOR A LONG STAY

A few weeks after we arrived, Santo Tomas Internment Camp had become overcrowded, and the housing situation would have to be corrected. At that time, the men in the group of American businessmen who had anticipated the Japanese occupation and prepared for it, were working as the internee administrators of the camp. Later, there were elections and a number of committees were set up to be responsible for every aspect of our lives, subject to the Japanese camp commander's direction or approval. He was initially an Army officer, but that position was subsequently turned over to a Japanese civilian from the diplomatic corps, supported by Japanese soldiers. We were never free of the presence of armed guards.

Our leaders decided to redistribute the housing for everyone. The Main Building and Annex were assigned as dormitories for the women and children, the Gymnasium became one huge dormitory for the men, and the Education Building upper floor was assigned to young single men and older boys. The Japanese administration used the lower two floors of the Education Building for housing, offices, and a guardhouse.

When the reassignments were made, my mother, sister, and I were assigned to a dormitory on the third floor of the Main Building, near the southeast corner overlooking the Education Building. After we moved in, we discovered that some men in the carpentry shop had made wooden cots for all of the people in our dorm. At first they were uncomfortable because they were just slats of wood on a base with short legs. But we were each assigned a blanket, which when folded and laid on the slats, softened them somewhat. In a short time, we became quite accustomed to sleeping on this hard mattress. We were also each given a mosquito net, which provided a modicum of privacy when draped over our cots, as well as protection from mosquitoes that swarmed as the weather grew warmer and damper.

Our dormitory was in a great location. From our window, we could see over the wall and across the city to the cordillera in the far distance. Just being able to see those far away mountains gave us a sense that the world did not end at the walls that surrounded us. And we could look into the windows on the end and down the length of the front of the Education Building, which was not important at that time, but later gave me a front-row seat to the events that happened in that building. In retrospect, that move from the west side of the building to the east side may have saved our lives as things later turned out.

Also, something had to be done about our food supply. The Japanese did not provide food for us, and required the internees to fend for themselves. Initially, the stockpile of food that the American businessmen had accumulated before the war was the basis for our meals. But this soon was depleted by the enormous influx of new prisoners. Then the Philippine Red Cross arranged to provide money for the camp to buy food, using funds that had been provided by the American Red Cross before the war. In camp, a committee was set up to procure food, and the Japanese allowed buying agents to go into the Filipino community to obtain food and have it transported into the camp.

To feed the growing number of internees, a central kitchen was set up between the Main Building and the Annex. Volunteers inside the camp ran the kitchen and served the food. When that operation was running smoothly, it started to serve three meals a day to everyone. It was simple food, mainly cornmeal and rice, with stews and soups. Serving 3,000 people three meals a day was an enormous undertaking, but with patience and standing in long lines, people got fed.

Not only was our living space and feeding reorganized, but also the camp leaders attempted to bring a sense of normalcy to our lives. Clubs were organized for such things as bridge, book exchanges, crafts, and sports. Entertainment, shows, and musical productions were staged. We had freedom to go anywhere on the campus, but there was a curfew, and we were required to return to our dormitories every evening to answer roll call.

I didn't realize it at the time, but there were really two classes of people in the camp. About half of the people formed the aristocracy. They were mainly Americans who had lived in Manila for a long time, had deep roots in the community, and had extensive contacts with friends, relatives, and servants, and other Filipinos outside the walls. These people were blessed because they could rely on their outside contacts to provide extra food and luxuries by passing packages through the fence. They had long-standing social groups that were in camp together. And the kids had their classmates with them, and even their teachers, so their education could continue almost seamlessly.

The under class were people who were transient in Manila, had been diverted there as a result of the war, and the military families whose fathers were gone to fight the Japanese. Without their contacts in the Filipino community, they had to accept what was provided in the camp, unless they had enough money to buy needed supplies from the aristocracy or on the black market. Many of these people did not have the money to supplement the official issue, and suffered as a result. Fortunately, my mother had drawn a considerable amount of cash from my father's company office in Manila to take care of our hotel bill and other incidentals, and still had quite a few Filipino pesos when we were brought into the camp. This money served to give us a slightly better life than most of the others in the under class.

Some of the people in the aristocracy used their access to goods and food from outside the camp to start little businesses. Some sold clothes or other items that had been given to them in packages, while others set up little food stands where they sold specialty foods. These stands were the most popular to people who had a little money because the food we were getting from the central kitchen was bland and uninteresting.

∞ ∞ ∞

My first run-in with the class system occurred shortly after the reorganization of the accommodations. There were other children in our dormitory and the adjacent ones, and when I tried to make friends, the American boys snubbed me and called me a lousy limey. The fact that I had an English accent and an attitude that probably came across as superior snobbism didn't help a bit. I asked my mother what a limey was, and she explained how English sailors for hundreds of years had eaten limes to ward off scurvy on long ocean voyages, and were thus called limeys. Well that was OK. If a limey was a brave English sailor I should be proud of that name. But the pejorative of being lousy wasn't very helpful in making friends.

Then to add insult to injury, I was standing in line for my meal one day when another boy asked if it was true that my dad had been shot by the British and put in a POW camp during World War I. I knew that both of these statements were true, but I didn't yet know the entire story and the reasons he became a British prisoner. I was unable to explain that my dad lived in the German Concession in Tientsin when that war broke out, and had tried to escape so that he could go to his job with an American company, when he was shot and put in a POW camp. But the British released him so that he could join the American Army, and he served in France, where he received a battlefield commission. Had I been able to give this full explanation, I would have skated through the confrontation. But honestly, I could only admit that the boy's contentions were true. So now I was tagged as not only a lousy limey but also a crummy krauthead.

These incidents made it difficult for me to make friends with the Americans who were the same age as me, and I hadn't discovered any other British boys my age. This left me pretty much on my own resources, and I was lonely in the middle of a sea of humanity.

A number of families had brought pets into camp with them, and my mother agreed to let my sister and me have one of the kittens from a litter born in camp. On the day that we took the kitten to our dormitory, my mother arranged a special treat. We went to one of the entrepreneurs who had acquired a waffle iron, and bought a waffle with syrup for each of us. After debating what name to give the kitten, we combined the two auspicious events of the day, and called her Waffles.

When the camp administrators started to organize sports programs, my mother suggested that I join a team. My favorite sports were swimming and diving, but there was no pool on the campus, so I arbitrarily signed up for baseball. It was a game about which I knew absolutely nothing, since I had never seen it played in Tientsin. That meant that I had to learn how the game was played and its rules. That was easy enough because everyone was assigned to a team based on age grouping, and we started to play on the field in front of the gymnasium.

It seemed to me that baseball was a very strange game, or at least the way we played it in Santo Tomas. You had two teams, one "at bat" and the other in the "field," and when three people were put out at bat, the two teams switched places. One of the people on the at bat team stood at home base with a bat and tried to hit a ball thrown at him by the pitcher on the field team. Meanwhile, the other members of the at-bat team lounged around on the grass out of the way. The wooden bat was so huge and heavy that when the batter swung it, he was usually displaced more than the bat. And the diameter of the bat was so small that it was very difficult to hit the ball, so the batter got to swing at it as many times as he wanted until finally he hit it.

In a circle around home plate were arranged three cushions, called bases, maybe 50 feet apart. In the middle of them stood the pitcher for the field team, who was usually replaced by one of the coaches after he had tried several times to throw the ball at the batter, and failed to get it close. Other members of the field team sat on the three bases, while more members lay in the grass out beyond them. When the batter finally hit the ball, he was required to run to the first base, and if a member of the field team stopped the ball that had been hit, and rolled it between the batter and the base, the batter was out. If no one rolled the ball before he reached the base he was safe, and now had to run to the next base if he could get there without someone rolling the ball between him and that base. If he got all the way around the bases back to home base, his team scored a run.

It seemed like a very strange game, but I hadn't yet learned to play cricket, which was the British equivalent of baseball, so I didn't really know what strange was. We played this game for a few months until the season was over, and the winning team was awarded a cup that had been artfully carved from a joint of giant bamboo, with pictures of our players sitting on the bases. I don't remember how my team stood in the rankings of our league because I really never knew who won each game. I suppose our coaches had some way of keeping score, but it was a mystery to me. The first time I saw a professional baseball game in America, there was a click in my mind as I realized, "That's what we were trying to do!" As mystified as I was at baseball, it had the salutary effect of putting me in the company of other boys my age, and I started to form a circle of friends.

The other sport that I joined was boxing. It was well-coached and I learned the basics of self-defense, which served me well later in life. For my age group, it was quite harmless and we concentrated on footwork and holding up our gloves in defensive maneuvers. The gloves were huge and our skinny arms didn't carry much of a punch, so it was like hitting each other with powder puffs. It was nothing like the blood sport that I encountered later when I was going to a British boarding school, or the street fights that I got into when I was in high school.

∞ ∞ ∞

Now that I was hanging around with the American boys, I started to lose my English accent, and I lost my reputation as a lousy limey. Being a crummy krauthead died of its own accord as I gained acceptance in my new crowd.

New adventures beckoned as I now roamed the campus with one or more friends. One of the things we discovered was a Catholic chapel at the end of the Seminary nearest the Main Building. Though the Seminary was out of bounds, the chapel was not, so a group of us went inside to explore it. I would never have done this on my own as I was awed by its religious significance to the Catholics, and being Episcopalian, I thought that I didn't belong there. But the other kids didn't have the same qualms, so in we went. I recall it being a beautiful little place, quiet and filled with peace. Later, I was quite upset by its violent destruction.

The most exciting thing we found was a museum that opened off the mezzanine just above the front lobby of the Main Building. The University had apparently specialized in biology and life sciences, and the museum was a showplace for specimens of animals. I could wander around the large hall for hours, gazing at some of the unique exhibits like a 60-foot python or a two-headed mouse. Never did I dream that sixty years later I would be honored at the ribbon-cutting ceremony when the main floor of the museum was dedicated to exhibits and photos of the Santo Tomas Internment Camp era.

I remember those first few months in Santo Tomas being relatively carefree. I'm sure that was not true for the adults, who wondered about how long we were to endure the confinement and what had happened to family and friends elsewhere. But we kids lived for the moment and adapted to our new environment almost seamlessly.

At first, we didn't even fear the Japanese guards, who we would see around the campus with their omnipresent long rifles. We would go up to them and chatter away, while they smiled and patted us on the heads. But that all changed after a couple of months. One night, three men climbed over the walls and escaped. They were only gone a day when they were recaptured by the Japanese in Manila and brought back to Santo Tomas.

Now began the first event that made us realize that the Japanese were not going to be benevolent captors. The men were tortured for three days in the Japanese jail, which was located in the guardhouse at the end of the Education Building. People who lived in the Education building said they could hear their screams as the guards inflicted extreme pain, for what purpose, no one knew. The Japanese just liked to hurt people who they were punishing. After being tortured, they were taken to the Manila North Cemetery, where they were made to dig their own graves. Some of the internee leaders were brought along as witnesses, and the prisoners were made to sit at the end of the holes, then shot in the back of the head and kicked into their graves.

Our relationship with the Japanese guards completely changed after that. Everyone in the camp now realized that this was not just a benign place to pass the time until we could again be free. We now realized that our lives were in deadly jeopardy, and our situation could well get worse before it got better. Though I didn't feel any fear, I now had a new respect for the rules in the camp, and assiduously obeyed them, even warning my friends when they seemed to be stepping out of line. This respect for rules was so inculcated in my mind that throughout my life I always tried to be law abiding, and when I broke even a traffic law, I had a sense of foreboding.

∞ ∞ ∞

Early in the spring, bad news started to filter into the camp, smuggled in packages passed through the fence from the outside community. The American and Filipino armies had surrendered on the Bataan Peninsula. Then details of the horrific Bataan Death March were smuggled in, and we learned that thousands of the surrendered soldiers had died. The morale of our community started to sink even further.

A month later, the surrender of Corregidor became known, and was confirmed when the Army and Navy nurses, who had been on the island with our troops, were brought into Santo

Tomas. The Japanese apparently did not consider them military personnel, and spared them the fate of the men who were captured, imprisoned under inhuman conditions, and shipped to Manchuria and Japan to work as slave laborers.

Now we knew that relief from our captivity was not close at hand. America was not going to ride to our rescue any time soon. We needed to make the best of what we had, to scrimp and save our food, clothing, and any other amenities that could not be replaced.

When questioned about camp conditions, the Japanese camp commander pointed out that Japan had not signed the Geneva Convention on the treatment of prisoners. Japan had its own rules that had been laid down in Tokyo for their treatment. And not a little of what came to pass resulted from the Japanese desire for revenge against the hated Westerners who they felt had treated them so shabbily in the past. At that time, we kids were blissfully ignorant of this background, but in the years to come, the Japanese philosophy on the treatment of prisoners would come to haunt us.

ELEVEN

AN ALTERNATE HELL

The warm and dryer Manila winter and early spring changed to a hot and wetter late spring and summer of 1942. Now the over-crowded conditions began to breed more serious diseases than the recurring dysentery that had plagued us since we arrived. Cases of dengue fever cropped up. It was often called break-bone fever because of the pains that racked the sufferer's body. Also, cases of malaria increased, and there was no way to hold down the mosquito population that bred in the swampy part of the campus and in the drainage ditches that laced the open land. The Infirmary had become a full-scale hospital with wards for those suffering from these and other diseases that afflicted us. Everyone in our family was lucky to dodge the mosquito-born diseases. I don't know why, because I remember being itchy with mosquito bites.

Unbeknown to my sister and me, my mother enrolled us in the Holy Ghost Children's Home. This was a convent where the sisters had agreed to take several hundred children from Santo Tomas and keep them in a healthier place than the over crowded main camp. My mother also thought that we would get a better education, which was important since we had already missed half of a school year.

My mother obtained a permit from the Japanese administration to allow her to take us to the convent. We went out of the front gate onto Calle España, the first time we had been outside the confines of the camp in five months. She waved down a taxi, and we loaded in for a relatively short ride to our destination.

As we traveled through the streets, it was difficult to believe that we were in a city at war occupied by the enemy. Many people were walking along the streets, numerous vehicles drove by, and shops were open. Manila did not look that much different from the way it had looked in the days before the occupation; in fact, it looked busier, with only an occasional Japanese soldier or military vehicle to confirm that this was no longer an American commonwealth.

The Japanese could afford to be openhanded with the Filipinos. Their military juggernaut was rolling through Southeast Asia, bringing Malaya, Burma, the Dutch East Indies and other countries into their sphere of influence with very little resistance from the West. Their only disappointment was the delay caused by the defense of Bataan and Corregidor, which had lost them the opportunity to invade Australia. They looked at themselves as liberators of the brown races, and if the Filipinos were still a little standoffish, they'd eventually come around to the Japanese way of thinking.

But with few exceptions, the Filipinos hated the Japanese. They knew that between 5,000 and 10,0000 of the Filipino Scouts who had been captured on Bataan with the American Army had died on the Death March. (No one knew the exact number because many of them escaped into the jungle along the route of march.) They were still dying as prisoners of war under inhumane conditions at Camp O'Donnell. Quietly, a resistance was being organized. Guerilla units, formed of escaped prisoners and new recruits, were organizing in the cordillera, and intelligence operatives were setting up networks and collecting information about the Japanese deployment and operations.

The Filipino resistance organizations were still ineffective, and there was no way that America could support or supply them, but eventually they would start to sting their country's occupiers. And when the tide of war changed, the Japanese would retaliate with such fury and viciousness against the Filipino people that their actions were condemned by world opinion and became a centerpiece for the war crimes trials that came after the war. But for now, all appeared placid in Manila.

∞ ∞ ∞

Our taxi turned in through a gate into a walled and tree-shaded complex that included several large buildings and a chapel. This was the Holy Ghost Convent, where my sister and I were now to be inmates. I had become comfortable and was enjoying life in Santo Tomas when my mother so rudely tore me out of what was becoming a familiar environment and put me into this foreboding place. The severe architecture of the buildings and groups of black-clad nuns strolling through the grounds reinforced my fears. Perhaps these fears were based more on the fact that I would be alone without my mother for the first time in my life, not on the newness of the place. I had transferred into the Santo Tomas campus without a problem. Whatever it was, the churning in my bowels signaled my foreboding as I wondered what was to come.

My mother left us with the nuns, and returned in the taxi to Santo Tomas. One of the nuns took my hand and led me to the dormitory where I would be living. She was Filipino and seemed quite nice, which took the edge off my discomfort. The dorm was a large room with cots lined up in military ranks, each covered with a mosquito net. She took me to one in the middle of the room and told me to leave my suitcase on it. She then led me to the dining hall for lunch.

Long tables, lined with rows of chairs on both sides, began to fill up with groups of kids being led in by nuns. I learned later that the groups were classes that stayed together through their meal periods. My table was soon filled, and I got to meet my new classmates. My sister, sitting at another table with older kids, seemed to be integrating easily into her class. But I felt a little awkward and shy.

At one end of the dining hall sat a group of nuns. I couldn't help staring at them because, for all the world, they looked like a bunch of crows to me. Their presence intimidated me. I did not understand why they dressed so funny, but I knew it had some important religious significance. I couldn't help but think of the story of Joan of Arc, who was condemned by the Catholic clergy, and then burned to death at the stake. I wondered if this black-clad coterie would sit in judgment of me if I did something wrong. Between the Japanese guards in Santo Tomas and the black-clad nuns, I was developing a real apprehension about authority figures. I barely said a word all through lunch, and my classmates didn't make much effort to draw me out.

After the meal, the nun who had taken me to my dorm reappeared with an older boy of about 13. She said that he was going to show me around the school so that I could get oriented, and the next morning, I should report to my classroom after breakfast. He seemed rather disinterested in his assignment, but he walked me through the grounds and pointed out the various buildings—where I'd be going to class, the chapel where I would go to church, and the forbidden areas where the nuns lived.

Perhaps I shouldn't have been surprised that a convent had become a children's home in these chaotic times. It was a logical place to house and educate children of the internees in Santo Tomas. Indeed, it was not far distant from the camp and had been an exclusive girl's school before the war. The facilities and faculty were already in place, just waiting for a new wartime mission.

The Holy Ghost Children's Home was the idea of Dr. Fe Del Mundo, a native of Manila who had done postgraduate work at Harvard University. She was the first woman admitted to the Harvard Medical School and had continued postgraduate studies at Columbia University and Mount Sinai Hospital. Subsequently, she completed her residency at the University of Chicago's Billings Hospital and then returned to Boston for a research fellowship at the Harvard Medical School Children's Hospital. Her studies were focused on children's diseases. Several of her patients' parents were interned at Santo Tomas.

After the Japanese invaded, she looked for opportunities to care for the children of the internees and opened the Children's Home in a small Red Cross building. When the facility became overcrowded, the Sisters of the Holy Ghost College agreed to house the internee children. Eventually, there were more than 400 children who had stayed at the Children's Home.

When I met this remarkable little sparrow of a lady again many years later, she was 94 years old and still doing research on children's diseases at the University of Santo Tomas. It was hard for me to believe that so many years earlier I had trepidations about staying in a home under her supervision. Dr. Del Mundo had spent her entire life working to better the lives of children.

∞ ∞ ∞

That first evening at the Holy Ghost, I lay in my cot finding it difficult to go to sleep. A nun was walking up and down the rows of cots, and when she came to mine, she asked how many times I had gone to the bathroom that day. The question put me in a moral dilemma. My bowel habits were not a subject that seemed proper to discuss with one of these people who shared the mantle with St. Joan. Moreover, what would the penalty be if I admitted that I'd been five times, though most likely as a result of nerves rather than dysentery? Should I answer truthfully, or should I lie?

I lay in the darkness feigning sleep while the black apparition hovered over me. My stomach started to churn again, and I wondered if I should surrender and make a dash for the bathroom. While I lay there clenching, she waited, then finally sighed and moved on to the next cot. When she was gone, I relaxed and the wave of bowel pain thankfully disappeared. I was then able to go to sleep and was greatly rested and more relaxed the next morning knowing that fate had intervened in my favor.

When classes started the next morning, I was shown where my classroom was located. I entered the classroom carrying the notebook, ruler, and compass that my mother had included in my suitcase when we left Tientsin. She had written my name in block letters on each of these items so that I wouldn't lose them. The teacher introduced me to the rest of the class, and then asked me to come to the front of the room and write my name on the blackboard.

I stood in front of the class and wrote my name in large block letters. When I finished, the girl sitting at the desk behind mine raised her hand, and the teacher recognized her. The girl stood up, and said, "He spelled his name wrong." The teacher asked how she knew that, and she said, "Its written right here on his ruler." I was totally embarrassed, and knew that I had now made an enemy for life. Of course at that age, a lifetime was about a week, and by then I'd forgotten this terrible slight, but at least I was more careful about spelling my name after that.

It didn't take me long to integrate into the class. I was probably more advanced in my studies than many of the other children, so it was not difficult for me to keep up with the lessons.

One of the most exciting things to happen was when a Japanese film crew set up in our classroom to take some pictures of our everyday life. We all behaved with exceptional decorum, and our serious demeanor was recorded on film. Little did we know that we were starring in a propaganda film that the Japanese used to show how well they were treating their Western guests in the occupied countries.

Many years later, I received some archival footage of Japanese propaganda movies, and much to my surprise, I discovered myself in one of those films. The camera panned across the classroom, then pulled into a close-up of me sitting at my desk, looking exceptionally studious. Never had I dreamed that I had helped the Japanese sell the idea that we were being well-treated. I don't know how much damage this propaganda did to our war effort, but I do know that films taken, and documents recovered after the Americans returned to Manila, refuted any lies that the Japanese had spread during a period that later had to be considered a honeymoon compared with what was to come.

∞ ∞ ∞

My memories of the Holy Ghost remain quite vague, aside from the few instances mentioned. I remember that I was not happy there. When my mother came to visit on those limited occasions when it was permitted, I complained to her that I didn't want to stay. She tried to comfort me, and told me to continue to try to adjust and everything would turn out all right. After all, my sister, Lucy, had adjusted well and was happy to stay as long as necessary.

What the source of my discomfort was is no longer clear to me, though I think it had to do with religious aspects of staying in the convent. Though there was no overt effort to convert us to Catholicism, everything was geared to Catholic ritual, saints' days, and attendance at the services in the chapel. At first, I didn't understand whether I should wash my hands in the font outside the chapel, drink the water, or dip my hand and make a sign of the cross. By watching others, I caught on, but what was the significance of touching your forehead, chest, and shoulders with the holy water?

Had I been a little older, I might have adopted the ritual, and who knows, maybe even become a Catholic. But at my age, everything was so foreign that it merely made me apprehensive. It seemed like everything was aimed at punishing sinners, and I was scared that I might do something that would earn me the punishment of their wrathful God. What I could remember of my Episcopal upbringing was that we seemed to have a much more gentle and loving God, and our pastor was a friendly, jolly, little man, unlike the severe and unapproachable priests who conducted the service in the chapel in a language that totally mystified me.

After several tries at trying to convince me to stay, my mother finally acceded to my wishes and agreed to bring me back to Santo Tomas. She wasn't worried about my sister, and they agreed that she would stay at the Holy Ghost. With time, Lucy would probably have converted to Catholicism, but my mother either didn't see the signs, or didn't care that much. But events conspired to prevent a prolonged stay for her at the Holy Ghost, and perhaps my mother already saw the inevitability of our changing situation.

TWELVE

THE FIRST YEAR ENDS

At the end of summer, 1942, I returned to Santo Tomas Internment Camp in a taxi with my mother, which let us out by the
huge wrought iron gate. We passed through it back into the campus, showing the armed sentry our pass. It was the last time I
would be outside the walls until the war was over for Manila in
another two and one-half years. A lot of things had changed during my three-month absence, some for the better and others
demonstrating the tighter control that the Japanese were exert-
ing over our lives.

The first thing I noticed was that the iron railing fence along
Calle España was now covered with sawali matting. No longer
could Filipinos pass packages to prisoners on the inside or to
sell food through the bars. Now all packages had to go through a
package station where the Japanese could open them and take
out anything that was prohibited. That meant that messages
were severely restricted, and our source of information about the
outside world, particularly the progress of the war, was cut off.
Fortunately, the Filipinos met the challenge and passed clandes-
tine messages by throwing them over the walls in remote locations. But what hurt me most was that I couldn't trot over to the
fence and buy a treat to supplement my lunch. Now the aristocracy had a monopoly on what could be bought and sold, creating
a black market.

Also, my mother told me that she had turned Waffles the cat loose. She told me that there was no way to keep the cat in the dormitory. We had little food to share with it. She was sure that it would do quite well on its own, as there were lots of rats and other rodents for it to eat. Perhaps it was a good thing that Waffles was gone, because it would have been unbearable to think of it suffering the same fate as so many other pets later did.

On the good side was that the Japanese administration had agreed to allow the internees to build shanties so that they had a place to go during the daytime other than the picnic areas or the overcrowded dormitories. Several large tracts of open space on the north and east sides of the campus had been divided into lots, and shanties had sprung up in a wild disarray of disparate architecture. My mother used some of her hoarded money to hire some men to build one for us. When she showed me our new daytime home, she was inordinately proud and I was wild with excitement.

The shantytowns were carefully laid out with paths so that none of the small plots were blocked in. Our shanty was located just off the northwest corner of the annex, with a main north-south pathway in front of it, and the main east-west pathway just one shanty to the north of us. The pathway in front ran along the edge of a large deep drainage canal, lined with blue clay and with a tropical redolence of stagnant water and rotting vegetation.

The shanty itself was about ten-feet square and built much like the village hut we had visited in Bataan, except that it was not raised in the air so it had a dirt floor, which was mainly mud during the rainy season. The structure was large diameter bamboo, with a roof of nipa that was about seven-feet high at the eaves and nine-feet at the peak. The rear wall was completely closed with sawali matting, and the two sides were sawali up to a waist high window level, and open above that. The front was mainly open with a bamboo railing across it next to the door opening. Next to the door stood a small full-height cupboard made of split bamboo and sawali.

My mother furnished the shanty with a canvas camp cot and two deck chairs. There was, of course, no running water, unless you counted me running over to a faucet in the annex with a bucket. And we still had to use the toilet facilities in the Annex and the Main Building. Our next-door neighbors were an English family with a son who was two or three years older than me, so I had a kindred spirit nearby. Oh, it was a lovely home, and I was just going to love it here.

Another improvement was the huge movie screen built at one end of the plaza. Every once in awhile, we were shown a movie acquired from a theater in Manila. I, along with everyone else, set up a blanket or chair in front of the screen in anticipation of a special entertainment treat. The movies were old, made in the 1920s and 30s, and the action had to be stopped to change reels since there was only one projector. Also, it seemed that the film would break at the most inconvenient places in the middle of the action, and then we would all have to sit around and wait for it to be spliced together. We were very impatient for the action to restart, but generally well-behaved and didn't make catcalls, which usually occurred if there was a problem in a real movie theater before we were interned.

The entertainment fare was quite varied, and the warm tropical evenings made our theater under the stars a delightful break from the tedium of our existence. I liked Laurel and Hardy, Marx Brothers, and a variety of other comedies. One time, Sigmund Romberg's operetta, "The Merry Widow", was shown. The girls just loved it and got all dreamy-eyed when they discussed how romantic it was. I liked it fine too, except for the mushy parts where the man and woman stood real close together and sang how they loved each other only.

The movies were just part of our entertainment. Clubs had been organized to present little plays and choral events. People had time on their hands, and they used it creatively to make life more pleasant for everyone in the camp. Especially in the first couple of years, there was a lot of activity to give the internees a meaningful life. But I enjoyed the movies best and still remember the plots of some of them.

∞ ∞ ∞

It was a sort of birthday present that my mother had brought me back from the Holy Ghost, and in August on my seventh birthday, she gave me another special treat. One of the entrepreneurs, who had access to packages from outside, had a little stand near our shanty where he cooked eggs for those who had the money to pay for them. On my birthday, my mother gave me the money to buy breakfast, and I had a fried egg and toast. In my mind I can still taste that delicious egg because it was so special, and it was the last fresh egg I was to have for almost three years.

I still had the notebook my mother had given me to take to the Holy Ghost, and now she suggested that I start to write down everything that had happened to us since we left China. That was a good project to keep me occupied, and I carefully printed, with a pencil, my version of our trip to Hong Kong, then to Bataan, our stay in Manila, and then how we were brought to Santo Tomas. My notebook eventually disappeared, so that version is no longer available to me, except the process of writing it down served to imprint those events clearly in my mind to be regurgitated in this tome. I suspect that my mother later destroyed the notebook when the Japanese administration threatened severe penalties for anyone who was keeping notes about life in their exemplary paradise.

As the new school year started in Santo Tomas, I was enrolled in the second grade of what was characteristically an American school. Our classes were held in classrooms located on the roof of the Main Building. These were low lying, and could barely be seen from the ground because of the parapet around the edge of the roof.

The first day I reported for class, I discovered that there were about twenty students in my class, and we were to take desks that were arrayed in several rows facing the teacher's desk and a blackboard, typical of most formal classrooms. I sat at a desk near the back of the class so that I wouldn't be too prominent to the teacher and other students. But after the initial period, when the teacher asked everyone to introduce themselves, she asked me to sit in the front row next to a boy with a dark complexion.

When there was a recess, she asked the two of us in the front row to stay for a moment. After the other students had left, she told me that she wanted me to be the friend of the dark boy and introduced him as Alonzo. That was fine with me. Alonzo was American, and though my English accent was slowly disappearing, it was still difficult to make friends with the American boys. She told me later that Alonzo was a bit wild, and she thought that pairing him with me would help calm him down.

Alonzo and I became best friends. We would play together all the time. He was with me when I received my first "identifying" scar, one that I could use later in life on documents that required specific characteristics that could be used for positive identification. We were playing on a large coke pile behind the Main Building that was used for the fires in the main kitchen. At the top, I slipped and fell down the face of the pile, gashing my knee. The black carbon from the coke filled the gash, and when I went to see a doctor, he couldn't clean it all out. When the gash healed, the scar tissue had a black cast to it. Amazingly, that black scar is no longer there today, the carbon being finally absorbed and other scars covering that original one.

There were many other adventures that Alonzo and I shared, but that was the only one that left an indelible mark on my body. I'm not sure what the teacher meant when she told me that Alonzo was wild. He seemed like just another normal exuberant kid to me. But the teacher told my mother that I had done wonders to calm him down.

I didn't understand what the problem had been until more than sixty years later when I was at a reunion of people who had been in Santo Tomas and met Virginia Glass. Virginia, I found out, was half African-American and half Filipino, and when I was chatting with her, I asked why her name seemed so familiar. She tried a few different associations, but none of them worked, and I figured it was just my mind playing tricks on me. Then she mentioned that perhaps I had known her little brother, who would have been in my class. His name was Alonzo. Suddenly the connection was made, and after thinking about it, the reason for Alonzo's so-called wildness became clear.

The American residents of Manila in the 1940s were a microcosm of America. Prejudice against Negroes ran deeply in the American psyche. Alonzo wasn't "wild'. The other boys were simply discriminating against him. Then along came a British boy from China who had never been inculcated with this racial hatred, and the teacher saw an easy way out. By pairing him with me, she eliminated his loner status and put him in a relationship where he could behave like a normal kid. And what was really strange was that I never thought of him as being anything other than a regular kid, let alone a Negro.

After I made this connection, I became alert to the nuances that were present with others during the reunions I attended. I became aware that many of them were victims of prejudice when they first entered Santo Tomas. Certainly I was, Alonzo was, and the Chinese were, as were many others of mixed races. But it is one of the great strengths of Westerners, and Americans in particular, that when the times become difficult, petty differences are set aside and they all pull together. Though there may have been class and racial differences in the first months and years after we first entered the internment camp, they were swept aside as we were faced with the greater challenge of survival. It was then that the tales of mutual support and individual sacrifice showed the true color of our collective soul.

∞ ∞ ∞

At the end of October, when mail was brought into the camp, we received a special treat. The mail had come from America on the *Gripsholm*, been transferred to the *Teia Maru* during the first prisoner exchange in June of 1942, then eventually had made its way to Manila, where it was censored by the Japanese before being distributed. The letters were now more than six months old.

My mother received a letter from someone at the home office of my father's company in New York. She had hoped it would provide information about my father and my brother, but the information available was negligible. The censors had used a razor blade to excise information that was restricted from the letter, so it looked like a Swiss cheese. Since the letter was handwritten on both sides, a censored part on one side resulted in part of the text on the other side also being lost. It was difficult to gain any continuity from the writing, but my Mother was able to ascertain that my father was still in Tientsin and was well as of the last available information about him. But there was no information about my brother. The letter did give a boost to our morale, as we now knew that we had friends thinking of us, and the information about my father was encouraging, though the lack of information about John was worrisome.

When Christmas of 1942 approached, there was a flurry of activity as people prepared for our first holiday season as prisoners. Those with craft skills made presents to be given away by Santa Claus, and the theater and choral clubs prepared entertainment programs. Under the tutelage of our teacher, my class started to rehearse a skit to be presented at a children's program.

Our number involved everyone in the class dressed as pirates, shaking ersatz pistols, and singing a pirate song. During our rehearsals in the classroom, we formed a V opening towards the audience, and my position was at the open end of one of the legs. We sang lustily and shook our pistols vigorously, and if our singing was off key, it was at least loud and enthusiastic.

On the day of the Christmas program, we waited off stage as other classes put on their acts, until it was our turn to take the stage. We trooped on and formed our V, except that the stage was backwards from our classroom, and we had our backs to the audience. Our teacher rushed onstage and herded the open end closed and the closed end open so our V now faced the audience. The only problem was that we hadn't rehearsed our skit this way, and now I was at the sharp end of the V with the kid across from me beating my hand to death with his pistol. Our class sang lustily, except for me, who let out a yelp at every beat as my opponent smacked the hard wood of his pistol across my knuckles. I suppose I could have stepped back out of the line of fire, but the show had to go on. The audience was polite and applauded us, but I stumbled offstage holding a bruised and bleeding hand, and so ended my budding career in show business.

That was the highlight of my Christmas. A man dressed in a rather pathetic Santa Claus suit handed out the hand-made presents to the younger kids, but I was now one of the cognoscenti, and much superior to the little kids who still believed in Santa, so I didn't participate. My mother and I had a quiet celebration of our own at our shanty, with a tree branch and paper decorations for our tree, and a special treat to eat. The kitchen served a special meal with a little more of the meat that had been hoarded, and a sweet treat was made with raw sugar that had been procured by the camp buyers. So Christmas turned out to be a special day after all.

The New Year came in with little note, and we were all confined to our dormitories at midnight, so there was no "seeing in the New Year." A few days later, we celebrated our first full year in Santo Tomas. It had been a long year for me, as time moves at a much slower pace for children, but it had not been unpleasant. I had faced many new experiences and had all kinds of adventures, and if life was a little restricted, it really didn't affect my world all that much. The food could have been better, and I didn't realize it at the time, but the lack of certain essential nutrients was slowly having an affect on my body. In the months to come this would start to have a cumulative effect on everyone, accelerating physical debility, in many cases to an ultimate collapse.

THIRTEEN

THE KNOT TIGHTENS

A few days after the start of 1943, camp leaders distributed a Red Cross package to everyone. We called the packages "comfort kits"; they were about the size of a double shoebox. Inside were a variety of canned meats, such as Spam, corned beef, and Vienna sausages, powdered milk, jam, dehydrated potatoes, biscuits, and other specialty foods such as tropical butter that could only be melted with a blowtorch. Also there were some personal items such as soap, cigarettes, and a cellophane bag of hard candies. The candies had long ago melted and congealed into a solid mass, but that didn't make any difference to me as I pulled off sticky lumps and sucked on them. What was even better was that I was able to trade my cigarettes to my mother for her bag of candy, and we were both more than pleased with the transaction.

We learned that the packages had arrived the previous summer aboard the *Teia Maru*. When the prisoner exchange was being made, the *Gripsholm* crew had transferred Red Cross packages, along with the mail that we had received earlier, to the *Teia Maru*, which then transported them to Manila. After holding the packages for several months, the Japanese finally distributed them at a good time to brighten our New Year.

We had now been in Santo Tomas for a full year, and still more people were arriving from distant parts of Luzon and from other islands. The camp became more and more crowded, even though the Japanese had let some of the elderly and sick people return to their homes; other sick were being treated in hospitals in Manila. Although 1942 had been uncomfortable and unpleasant for all of us, but not dangerously so, our spirits were good. But with the new year, we were about to face new challenges.

The cost of food in Manila was increasing, making it ever more challenging for the camp buyers to obtain enough to feed us using the small stipend that the Japanese provided for each prisoner. When we had originally arrived in Santo Tomas, the Philippine Red Cross had been providing $0.55 a day per person to feed us and pay for sundries. But after the Japanese confiscated their money and took on the responsibility of paying the stipend, they dropped it to $0.35 a day, and half that amount for children under twelve. The stipend also had to pay for utilities, sanitation, construction, medical supplies, and maintenance. So as inflation affected the costs, the amount and quality of food we received declined. Fortunately, our leaders had foreseen the food shortage and had prepared a plot of land for growing vegetables. From that garden, we harvested a few greens to supplement what was purchased outside the camp.

Long ago, the condensed milk we had received for our breakfast mush had been consumed. No dairy products were available at all. To compensate, our camp leaders purchased loads of coconuts and had them squeezed for their milk, which was primarily reserved for the children. A crew of men cracked and scraped the meat out of the coconuts for the grinding and squeezing operation at a nipa-roofed shed built between the Annex and the Infirmary. I, along with other kids, would hang around the shed, and once in awhile one of the men would slip me a small piece of coconut meat to chew on. On one occasion, they also received a load of sugar cane to squeeze for its sweet juice, slipping some of us kids a small piece to shred and chew for our own sweet treat.

∞ ∞ ∞

Between the comfort kits and those occasional purloined treats, eating was not a major issue for me, though I did look askance at the green leaves from the vegetable garden that I found floating in my soup. However, though I didn't recognize it, the meals lacked the proper nutritional balance. I was a growing boy and my baby teeth were in the process of being replaced by adult teeth. My body needed calcium to build healthy bones and teeth, and it was almost totally lacking in my diet. Later, from the time I entered High School, I had an inordinate problem with my teeth, something that didn't affect my sister, since her adult teeth had grown in while we still lived in Tientsin.

As the amount and quality of food continued to decline, my body adjusted by ceasing to grow. On both my father and mother's sides of the family, the men all stood over six feet tall, yet later, when I gained my full adult height, I was several inches below that standard.

Other nutrients were needed to stave off pellagra and beri beri. Fortunately, the camp medical staff had a small supply of a medicine called "tiki tiki." Through 1943, the nurses gave me regular doses of this sweet brown medicine, which I believe was made from rice hulls normally polished off the rice we received with our meals. When the medicine ran out, I was subject to the same nutrient deficiencies as the adults who had not received it. However, that extra couple of years of protection saved me from a severe case of beri beri, a malnutrition disease that affected practically everyone and became a major cause of deaths during the last months of our confinement.

One of the effects of beri beri was to cause scar tissue on the valves of a person's heart. When I was in high school, my physical exams would usually indicate a heart murmur, which the doctors attributed to beri beri. Over the years, different doctors detected that murmur and interpreted it differently, some with concern and some without. However, the Navy did discharge me early because of it. My present doctor told me that it should not be a worry; my aortic valve could be replaced by a pig's valve if leakage became a problem. In that event, my biggest concern is if a woman calls me a pig, she will be at least partially right.

The camp's internee doctors and nurses worked diligently and had lots of challenges. Cases of dysentery and enteritis continued to be high, and cases of malaria and dengue fever also cropped up. There were a few cases of diphtheria, which could be fatal, and whooping cough and measles arrived in epidemic proportions. The number of tuberculosis patients continued to grow, and fluoroscopic tests for tuberculosis showed an increasing number of children were testing positive because of the crowded conditions. Several years later when I came to America, I was given a chest x-ray and duly received notice that it was positive for tuberculosis. At that time, there was no successful treatment for the disease. Luckily, a retest indicated I was clean. For the rest of my life, tests never showed any indications of tuberculosis. I was fortunate to dodge this unpleasant and possibly fatal disease.

We were very fortunate in Santo Tomas to have the best of medical professionals to take care of us. When we were interned, the Western doctors in Manila, most of them Americans, were interned with us. Then in March of 1942, twelve Navy nurses were brought into the camp. In July, 72 Army nurses from Corregidor arrived. That gave us an adequate medical staff to look after our infirmities, though the supply of medicine stockpiled before the war steadily diminished. When that supply was depleted, no more medicine could be obtained unless it could be smuggled into camp, which became increasingly difficult.

∞ ∞ ∞

By early 1943, I was well-accepted by the other boys of my own age. We ran in packs of five or six and found fun, or trouble, where we could. One thing we had learned was to stay away from the Japanese guards, and if we saw any coming, we quickly disappeared in a different direction.

Our standard uniform was a pair of shorts, without shoes or shirt, so we were well tanned, and looked like a bunch of savages. School took up half our day, but we had plenty of free time. Our freelance games included kick the can, pile-on, hide and seek, and many other typical games for children of our age. One time we built a volcano by using clay mined from the drainage ditches, coiling it into a cone, then lighting a fire inside to produce smoke and steam. In an area of marshy ponds behind the Infirmary, we built dams and drained small ponds by bailing them with a cup, catching the small fish as the water drained away.

Another time, a large pile of firewood, perhaps 10-feet high, was randomly dumped between the Annex and the Infirmary. We discovered how to work out lengths of wood from the bottom of the stack and build tunnels into it. We soon had a warren of tunnels and chambers buried deeply under the stack. The adults watched in amusement, and no attempt was made to stop us. It was a wonder that the whole stack didn't collapse, creating a crisis with injured and dead little boys. Luckily, the central kitchen needed the wood for its open-air cooking fires, and the stack soon disappeared before any irreparable harm could be done.

My mother acquired a small clay cooking stove and a clay pot, which she used to make tasty supplements to our bland meals. She had carefully squirreled away most of the cans of food from our comfort kits. Then, through the black market, she obtained some soybean meal. She mixed the corned beef with the meal and baked it for a long time until it was very dry and hard. She called these little biscuits "hardtack" and stored them in a tin box. They were not to be eaten now, but to be saved for an emergency. Occasionally, we got one as a special treat, or my mother would open one of her saved cans of meat for a special celebration. The far-sighted camp leaders had advised people to save any preserved food from our comfort kits. They foresaw the difficult times that surely must lie ahead, when the fortunes of our Japanese captors were no longer so rosy, and they started taking out their anger on us.

She also used the soybean meal to make mush. This she spread out in a thin layer until it congealed, then she cut it into squares and fried it, using that almost unmeltable butter from the comfort kits. It was wonderful to have one of these little biscuits to help fill our stomachs on those days when the meals were inadequate and had not sufficiently reduced our gnawing hunger. She soon ran out of the butter, and then discovered that she could use Pond's Cold Cream for cooking. The perfume in this cosmetic left a strong flavor in the biscuits, but it was edible, and we weren't going to turn down food just because it tasted funny. For years later, the smell of that certain perfume would make me feel slightly queasy.

My mother needed fuel for the cooking that she did with her little clay pot. My job was to collect scraps of wood and branches for the fire, and I would range around the campus looking for anything that would burn. The main source was tree branches from the grove of trees between the plaza and the front gates. But other people were also cooking in their shanties, so the supply steadily diminished.

My mother came up with the idea of using the charcoal left after she had finished cooking to make briquettes. I was assigned to mine some clay out of the drainage ditch in front of our shanty and to crush the charcoal and mix the two together. This experiment wasn't a great success because the briquettes were difficult to light and wouldn't stay lit. That meant it was back to foraging for wood again.

I had to climb the trees to break off dead branches because no branches were left on the ground. One day, I climbed a large tree located between the Annex and the Infirmary and was reaching out to grab a dead branch about 20-feet up. I lost my balance, and fell. I can remember that fall as if it was in slow motion. I was going down head first, and landed in a crotch in the trunk just below me. My body rotated around my head, and I continued to fall, finally landing squarely on my bottom with my hands below me to brace the impact. I was undoubtedly lucky that my hard head had not lead me all the way down to the ground. Still, my dignity was injured, and I hoped that no one had noticed my accident.

I found the dead branch that I had been reaching for on the ground nearby, so I picked it up as the consolation prize and headed back for our shanty. On the way, I noticed that my hands were hurting and my wrists starting to swell. The pain was strong enough that I thought it best to tell my mother what had happened. She immediately took me to the clinic in the nearby Annex, where the doctor looked at my wrists, then took me to the fluoroscope to examine them.

I wonder why we had a fluoroscope, not just that there was one in Santo Tomas, but that it was so conveniently located. Now I believe that it was because the University had concentrated on life sciences, and the Annex was where the animal laboratories had been located. Anyway, the examination showed that both of my wrists were broken.

The doctor splinted and taped up my wrists, then put both arms in slings. That night, the pain finally started, and both of my wrists ached unbearably. The only relief I could get was aspirin, and it got me through the night, after which the pain became more tolerable and disappeared completely in a couple of days. Now I started to recognize the benefits of having both arms in slings, aside from the sympathy it generated with everyone who saw me. But with neither arm free, I couldn't do any work or chores. In class, I couldn't use a pencil to do homework or take tests, so for a few weeks I was excused from some of the onerous parts of my schooling. When the splints came off, the school year was just about over, and my newly healed wrists were in fine shape for the summer activities with my gang.

∞ ∞ ∞

In the spring of 1943, we had good news. My mother was called to the administration office, where she was told that we were on a list of people who may be included on the next prisoner exchange. She discovered that my father's name was also on the list, and he would board the repatriation ship in Shanghai. This was good news on two points, first that we may soon be getting out of Santo Tomas, and second, that my father was still alive and healthy somewhere in China.

I was very excited about the prospect of repatriation, not just because it would get us out of Santo Tomas, but because it would mean another sea voyage and the opportunity to see America for the first time. The days dragged as we waited for confirmation that we would be leaving. But then one day, my mother returned to our shanty and told me that we were no longer on the list to leave. She didn't know why we had been taken off, but said it was probably because all of the rest of the prisoners to be exchanged were American and we were not.

That was a personal tragedy for us, but another more general one also occurred. The Japanese had been reviewing the records of all of the men in the camp, and now suddenly rounded up those who had been military reservists or had some connection with the military before the war. We heard that they were being taken to Fort Santiago, which was headquarters for the Japanese secret police, the Kempetai, where they would be interrogated. After 60 days in this gloomy fortress, they were transferred to the Bilibid prison, which was being used for POWs. We now had another bunch of children, like the military families earlier, whose fathers had disappeared.

The families who had lost parents because they were in the military would not know until the end of the war what happened to them. If they had survived the fighting on Bataan or Corregidor, they became prisoners of war, and the prognosis for POWs was not good. Of those Americans who surrendered on Bataan, 80 percent were dead by the end of the war. The prisoners taken at Corregidor and other places in the Philippines, such as Santo Tomas, had it only slightly better because a third of them died as prisoners of the Japanese.

∞ ∞ ∞

In the summer, we were told the Japanese had decided to move all of us from the Santo Tomas campus to a new camp about 40 miles south of Manila at the University of the Philippines forestry field station at Los Baños. The camp had dispatched a number of men to Los Baños to start building barracks-style buildings from nipa, sawali, and bamboo. When we were told that everyone would be moving there, my mother arranged to have my sister, Lucy, return from the Holy Ghost so we could prepare.

Conditions at Los Baños were more primitive than they were at Santo Tomas. The field station was located adjacent to a small village on the shore of a huge lake called the Laguna de Bay at the foot of a heavily forested dormant volcano. It had few permanent buildings. Our leaders realized how difficult it would be to house, feed, and care for what would eventually amount to about 5,000 people, and they strenuously argued with the Japanese administrators that we should remain in Santo Tomas.

Eventually, the Japanese agreed that the Los Baños camp would be inadequate for the number of people they proposed to put there. Instead, they told our leaders to decide who would make the move. This was an opportunity for many in the under class to get more equitable treatment. In Santo Tomas, they could not afford to buy extra rations through the package line or the black market, nor could they afford to build shanties. The volunteers hoped a transfer would result in equal treatment for everyone.

Over the next few months, people started to leave Santo Tomas, and, in time, more than 2,000 people were transferred to Los Baños. Those of us who stayed, hardly felt any reduction in the overcrowding, because new prisoners were constantly being transferred in from other parts of Luzon and from other islands in the Philippines. Eventually, about 3,800 people were settled in Santo Tomas and 2,200 in Los Baños.

∞ ∞ ∞

During that summer, I turned eight years old. It was a day much like any other—hot, humid, with occasional rain that felt like a warm shower. I had no compunction about being out in the rain, because it was not uncomfortable, it washed the dust and dirt off me, and I dried quickly. Although there was no special celebration, my mother gave us an extra treat of a perfume-laden biscuit in a little ceremony in our shanty and opened a small can of Vienna sausages from her hoard.

School started again in September. I was now in the third grade. It wasn't that much different from the previous year, and the routine just became an integral part of my life. Food rations continued to be reduced, but children still received preferential treatment, and the size of our stomachs reduced gradually to the point we hardly felt hunger pangs. I don't remember much reduction in energy level, though it was obvious that we were becoming thinner.

The school year was again interrupted because my sister caught the measles, and I was quarantined. She was committed to a ward in the Infirmary, where she wasn't allowed visitors, except for my mother. She was there for a week before she could come home, and then to compound my mother's problems, I got the measles. I was also shunted off to the Infirmary, and before I knew it, was ensconced in a dark ward. Measles reputedly could affect your eyes, so the light level in the ward was kept quite low, which meant there was nothing the patients could do to pass the time—no games, no reading, no playing around. I really didn't feel sick, just itchy, but I was told not to scratch. I was in the ward for a week also, which was probably the longest week of my stay in Santo Tomas. The compensation was that the food was quite an improvement over that we were doled out in the food lines for our standard meals. We were told that we needed the added nutrition to help us back to health more quickly, and I wasn't about to complain about that. In fact, I was disappointed when I had to go back to our standard rations, wondering what those bits and pieces were in the so-called soup or stew.

The summer had brought several typhoons, with their heavy rain and flooding. But in November an unseasonable and fierce typhoon hit Manila, causing flooding throughout the city and within the Santo Tomas campus. As the storm raged, we were confined to our dormitory and helplessly watched the water rise. We were worried about our shanty, which would have little protection from the gale, and wondered what the floodwaters were doing to the structure, our belongings, and the food we had stored in the cupboard.

Finally, the storm passed, and my mother couldn't wait for the water to recede before going to our shanty to assess the damage. I accompanied her as we exited from the rear door of the Main Building and slogged through a foot of water across the street to the Annex. The Annex floor was above water, and we walked to the end nearest our shanty. At the exit, the stairs descended into the floodwaters, and we followed them down until the water was waist deep on my mother and chest deep on me.

It was only a hundred yards from there to our shanty, and my mother pushed intrepidly forward through the water. I could barely walk, and followed her half swimming and half pushing myself along with my legs. I had always loved swimming and this was great fun. To add to the adventure, floating islands of agglomerated sawdust drifted by. The site of Santo Tomas had been a sawmill before the University took over the property, and now the wood waste was rising to the surface.

In a short time, we arrived at our shanty and discovered that it was still standing with about two feet of water inside. My mother loaded me, then herself, with valuables from the cupboard, primarily food and that precious tin box of hardtack. We slogged our way back to the Annex and then to the Main Building, satisfied that the storm had done no great harm. It was then that my mother was told that the floodwaters contained sewage from all around the city, and we could be infected with typhoid and other disagreeable diseases. She immediately sent me to the shower room with one of her last pieces of precious soap and strict instructions to scrub myself all over and in every crevice.

Apparently the scrubbing was effective and neither of us came down with anything noxious. But for the remainder of my time in Santo Tomas, I remembered that adventure with great affection; it was the only time since our sojourn in Bataan that I had been able to frolic in water to my heart's content. My next opportunity to be fully immersed in water wouldn't come for another year and a half.

∞ ∞ ∞

Christmas soon rolled around again, and the people in Santo Tomas again made a special effort to enliven the holiday season with entertainment and parties with homemade gifts. Most welcome was another distribution of comfort kits that had been brought to Manila after the second exchange of prisoners. My father had been on that exchange between the *Teia Maru* and the *Gripsholm*, but we had no way of knowing that.

This time, we were each given only half of a Red Cross food package instead of the full one that had been shipped to us. The Japanese had diverted half of the shipment for themselves. In addition, before turning the packages over to our camp leaders, they had opened all of them and removed the cigarettes. This was a great blow to the smokers, which included most of the adults. Still, the comfort kits were most welcome, and my mother had an opportunity to restock her supply of hardtack, which had been depleted during the year. She also put away the few other cans of meats and specialties that came with the packages.

Our special treat on Christmas day was to have a larger than normal ration for Christmas dinner, though it was the same old so-called stew. But my mother supplemented this by opening a can of Spam. She cut the little loaf in half, carefully storing one of the pieces for our New Year's treat. She cut the other piece into three parts and fried them in cold cream. Our little family celebrated with this veritable feast of sickly stew and perfumed pork.

We heard that some of the Aristocracy, who had surreptitiously brought ice cream into the camp, had much more elaborate feasts than we did. But it was only a rumor. We could hardly be jealous if we didn't see them actually eating ice cream, a treat I had missed for almost two years.

Again the New Year passed with little note except to change the calendar, and again to supplement our soupy rations with the small pieces of perfumed Spam left over from Christmas. For sure, 1943 had been an increasingly more difficult year. Rations were reduced and almost everything became in shorter supply. Our morale was declining as the Japanese propaganda we received was all about their great naval victories over the Americans. How much longer were we to be kept here? How much worse could conditions get? We were about to find out how grim life could really become.

This photo of Angus was taken in 1943 in anticipation of repatriation that never occurred.

FOURTEEN

THE YEAR OF STARVATION

On January 6, 1944, one day after our second anniversary as prisoners, our situation turned really ugly. Santo Tomas Internment Camp officially came under the direct supervision of the War Prisoners Department headed by General Morimoto, and came under the control of the Japanese military police. Regular Army military guards started patrolling inside the camp. We had always seen guards around, but now they were much more obvious. General Morimoto ordered all shanties located near the walls to be raised, an inner fence to be built, creating a ten-meter exclusion zone next to the inside of the walls, and a one-meter high barbed wire fence constructed on top of the walls. New regulations completely isolated the camp from any contact with outsiders.

In a more ominous decree, we were told that the camp was not being operated under terms of the Geneva Convention, but under a separate set of rules and regulations laid down in Tokyo. Japan had never signed the Geneva Convention and, therefore, had no obligation to treat prisoners humanely as described in that document.

We were warned that we must show better respect for the Japanese. When approached by any soldier or officer, we were to stop and bow. We were instructed that the proper position to assume was to have our upper bodies parallel to the ground, feet together, and arms pressed tightly against our legs. Japanese guards directly supervised the twice daily roll calls. During roll calls, we were required to assemble in the hallway outside of our room in two rows against the wall. When the guards approached, our room monitor would give us the order to bow by saying, "One, two, three, bow", and we would all bow in unison.

Shortly after Santo Tomas had been established, elderly and sick people were allowed to return to their homes in the city. Now the Japanese required these people to return, and all enemy aliens were held in the internment camp. The only way anyone was going to leave the camp was in the little pony drawn carriages that were used to carry people who had died out of camp for burial in one of the city's cemeteries. The little processions became increasingly common as the year wore on. Today, those same carriages are used in the Intramuros to take tourists for tours through the old city.

The Japanese also provided our food, rather than allow our camp buyers to continue to procure what we needed. They determined how much and what kind of food was to be provided; and until the army could start delivering it, we would have to live on what reserves our leaders had stored for us. When the army did start delivering food, it was consistently short of what was promised. The Japanese further threatened that in the case of American bombing of Manila, they would not be able to deliver food supplies.

As a result of these actions, our rations were cut immediately. And throughout the year, what we received for our meals was further cut, either by providing smaller portions, or by watering down what we were served. On top of that, the food we did get was very low quality, including such things as camote tops, the leafy top of this root plant, fish that was almost bad, and rice or ground corn that was full of weevils.

To further exacerbate the food shortage, the package line was canceled in January, so no supplemental food could be provided from friends outside of the camp. Now we were all in the same situation. No longer was there a class system, because money or outside contacts were no longer of value to the people who had been the aristocracy after the Japanese completely cut us off from the Filipino population. The only food we could get was what was served from the central kitchen, and it continually got pitifully less.

∞ ∞ ∞

Everyone's focus was on food. The evening meal was served at 5 o'clock, and I'd rush to stand in line by 4:30. Even then, there would be a lot of people in line ahead of me. When my bowl was filled in the food serving area, I'd carry it carefully back to our shanty. My mother and sister would join me, and we would slowly savor our meal. Actually, savor may be the wrong word. I was almost afraid to sort through any solid material in my "stew" in case I recognized it to be something disgusting.

The people occupying the shanty next to ours, a nice English family by the name of Honor, had a son about the same age as my sister. Their large shanty was set up on stilts about three feet above the ground. It was quite elegant. The Honors were good neighbors and always willing to pitch in when we needed any help. I became quite a close friend of their son, John, even though he was two or three years older than me. We shared a common heritage and were next-door neighbors.

They had a large dog they had brought into camp with them, and it slept under their shanty when we had to go back to our dormitories in the evening. One morning, John came over to our shanty and asked whether we had seen his dog. Since it was missing, I volunteered to go with him around the neighborhood and see if we could find their pet. Our morning of searching and asking people in other shanties if they had seen the dog was fruitless. But what was most disturbing was that several people had told us that they knew of people who were killing and eating the pets that people had with them. It seemed that my mother's release of the cat, Waffles, had been a good thing, as I wouldn't have to contemplate someone butchering and devouring it.

Now that I came to think about it, there were no longer very many cats and dogs roaming around the camp. It was easy to understand why the dogs were disappearing because there was no surplus food to feed them and they were becoming emaciated unless they escaped through the storm drains. However, the cats could sustain themselves on the rats and mice that proliferated around the drainage ditches and the camp vegetable gardens. As time went on, all of the dogs and cats disappeared, and it became an open secret who had captured and slaughtered one for their dining table.

In the spring, Alonzo and I had our big score. We had been scheming about how to supplement our food supply by capturing some of the pigeons that roosted under the eves of the Main Building. Obviously others had the same idea, because the size of the flock was steadily diminishing. We wanted to build a net that we could use, but string and other necessary supplies were just not available. Recognizing that deficiency, we turned our attention to the swampy ponds on the far side of the Infirmary.

We had been building dams and draining the smaller ponds to catch the small fish in them, but this was primarily a recreational activity. Now we decided to get serious and drain one of the larger ponds with the hope that we might find some larger fish. We launched our ambitious plan by building a mud dam of about six-feet in length across the end of a larger pond, then started to bail, each of us using tin cans that had previously held meat from our comfort kits. After hours of tedious bailing, the pond started to shrink in size, and we discovered a fish flopping around in the shallow water. It was a mud fish about four-inches long, an ugly creature that survived the dry season by burrowing into the mud and going dormant, but what a prize for us.

That evening, we both told our families that we were going to cook and eat the fish the next day. My mother was quite amused at this reversion to primitive life that I showed, and offered no criticism or suggestion. The next morning, Alonzo and I carried our very dead fish around the campus looking for a suitable place to build a little fire to cook it. We had no concept of how to clean a fish, and were just going to put the whole thing on a stick and roast it over the coals.

The longer we looked for a suitable place for our campfire, the greater the stench of the fish, which was rapidly decomposing in the tropical heat and humidity. It was so ugly, and now smelled so badly, that eventually we decided that we weren't yet that hungry. In the end, we took it back to the pond where we had captured it, and gave it a decent burial—ashes to ashes, mud to mud, and all that stuff.

On one occasion, the camp received a surplus of dilis, the small dried and salted fish that were used in the soups and stews cooked in the kitchens. These were trash fish rejected by the fisherman and about the size of goldfish. The surplus was put on a table behind the Main Building, and anyone who wished, could partake of them. I just happened to be in the area after the dilis were dumped out, so I went to the table and looked at the pile of raw fish baking in the sun. I was just hungry enough to try one.

I put a small fish in my mouth and found that it was like eating pure salt, which no fish flavor could overcome. I tentatively chewed it, and it wasn't bad, so I went ahead and ate the whole thing, head, fins, guts, tail and all. I then proceeded to eat three or four more of the fish, and probably would have stayed and eaten myself sick if the intense saltiness hadn't eventually driven me to find water. By the time I had slaked my thirst, word of the availability of this bonanza had become widespread, and the rest of the fish had been consumed. It was probably a boon for me, because hurling dilis would have been a most unpleasant experience.

∞ ∞ ∞

Manila now started to have routine air raid drills. We in Santo Tomas also participated and had to practice blackout procedures. This gave us a boost in morale since the Japanese had not felt it necessary to prepare for attacks in the previous years. It could only mean that the American forces were fighting back and beginning to threaten the Japanese domination of the Philippines. We had no idea how the war was going, and the sparse news that the Filipinos had been able to smuggle to us had dried up as the package line was shut down and the inner fence prevented messages from being thrown over the wall. Rumors, of course, were rampant, but there was no way of verifying them, and it seemed like a new one every day conflicted with the one on the previous day.

There were two levels of air raid alert. The first, a warning that an air raid was expected, was a rising tone of the siren, then held steady for several seconds, and then declining. This signal was repeated several times. When the actual air raid started, the alert would be a rapidly rising and falling tone of the siren, sometimes referred to as warbling. The all-clear signal was a single long blast of the siren. To this day, I never hear a siren without being transported back to those days when it had been a sound of hope.

We were warned ahead of time when a drill was to be held; and when the first warning signal was given, we would walk back to our dormitory, which was considered to be a safe place during a raid because it was a concrete building. Of course we were convinced that the Americans knew where we were and would not be bombing our camp, so the only protection we needed was from falling bomb fragments and shrapnel from the anti-aircraft fire.

From our dormitory window, we could see the blue mass of the Central Cordillera. Once in awhile, we would see clouds of smoke rising from somewhere in the mountains. People who claimed they knew told us that it was guerilla operations against the Japanese. Whether this was true or not, it served to keep our hopes up.

In September, the school year started again. I was now nine years old and in the fourth grade. Lucy was eleven and in the sixth grade. The classes were still being held in the rooms on the roof of the Main Building. Every day, we had to troop up the three flights of stairs, which was becoming increasingly more difficult as our nutrition continued to decline. But classes were serious, and we had to do our class and homework or risk failing grades.

On September 9, a first-level air raid warning sounded late in the afternoon, even though we had not been alerted ahead of time that there would be a drill. Was this the real thing? I went into the Main Building and joined other kids there. We were all excited that finally there was going to be some action, and we hovered around the windows hoping to see some American planes.

Some months earlier, I had traded some toy with another boy for his book on American fighting aircraft. It was a large book with full-page illustrations of flying aircraft, accompanied by a description of their capabilities. For instance, I found a picture of the P-40 that I had seen chasing the two Japanese Zeros that day so long ago when we had been in the garden of the British Embassy. The book had been published in 1941, and by that time, virtually all of the aircraft models that fought in World War II were either already in production or were in the proto-type stages, and so were illustrated in the book. I'm sure that if the Japanese had discovered it, they would have confiscated my book and probably severely punished me. They would have considered it strictly forbidden American war propaganda.

With that book, I was the center of attention as my friends gathered around, and we waited to see some of these planes in real action. However, not long after the warning alarm, the air raid siren again sounded. Within a few seconds, we groaned with extreme disappointment. It was not the warbling sound of imminent attack, but the single long drawn out wail of the all clear signal.

During the morning of September 21, less than two weeks later, we were in class when the warning siren sounded again. Just as we'd been trained in the air raid drills, our teachers herded us across the rooftop to the stairwell, and we went down into the safety of the concrete structure. Almost immediately, the warbling siren alarm for an immediate attack sounded. This time it was the real thing!

It is impossible to describe the leap of hope and excitement that this sound brought. I stayed on the third floor, which was as high as I could go without returning to the roof, and soon heard the "crump" of bomb explosions and the higher pitched explosions of anti-aircraft fire coming from the west side of the building. I walked around the connecting corridors and entered one of the dormitories on that side of the building. A group of people were standing back from the windows looking out. No one was right at the window, because we had been warned that we would be severely punished if we were caught looking out during an air raid, so everyone was far enough back to be able to look out without being seen from the ground.

I joined the group and edged into a position where I had a clear view. The window looked towards the harbor, which was about two miles away. In between were some buildings that blocked the view of the actual water, docks, or ships. What we could see, however, was very heartening. The sky over the harbor was blossoming with the black puffs of anti-aircraft explosions, just like that first day we had seen Manila as our ship approached from the bay. Now we prayed that the explosions were not harming our own aircraft, which we could occasionally see diving through the exploding flack.

The planes seemed to go into a vertical dive, then at the last moment, pulled out and climbed away at a steep angle, leaving behind an explosion in their wakes. At that distance, the bombs and anti-aircraft explosions were quite muted, but each bomb blast was clearly audible, and we hoped that it had sunk a ship or damaged some important Japanese military installation. The raid was quite short, and the aircraft soon disappeared. However, the all-clear signal did not sound, and throughout the day, there were several more raids.

I pulled out my book of airplanes, and people crowded around to see what kind had been attacking the harbor. Even men joined our crowd. We flipped through the pages, and found what we thought must be the planes. They had been fairly far off, so we had to guess from the silhouettes what we had seen. It looked like they were Navy SBD Douglas Dauntless dive-bombers, and the description fit what we had seen out of the window. Now the men got really excited and said that they were short-range aircraft, which meant the Navy had a fleet in the vicinity. Also, they said that the Americans wouldn't be bombing shore installations unless they were planning a landing somewhere in the Philippines and wanted to suppress the Japanese capability to fight back. What a boost to morale this raid had given us, and we now looked forward to more raids.

We were rewarded the next morning when the planes returned in several more successive raids. This time, some of the planes flew by near the camp, and we could confirm that they were the Navy dive-bombers we had identified in the book. We could soon see fires burning in the city, but aside from the harbor, we had no idea what other targets the bombers were hitting. But some of the men told us that they would be hitting Japanese airfields and command and control centers.

The Japanese now became quite jumpy, because air raid warnings were sounded several times in the next few days, but to our disappointment, no more planes arrived. Because of the warnings, lunch was not served on these days, and we had to wait a long time from breakfast to dinner. My mother now had a good justification for having hoarded food and making hard tack, because she doled these biscuits out to help us get through the day when we had no meal. The good news was that school was out as long as we were under an air-raid warning. We weren't confined to the Main Building when only the warning signal had been given, so I was free to roam outside. But when the air-raid alert sounded to warn us that an attack was imminent, everyone was supposed to immediately get into a shelter.

After a few days of warnings, things calmed down, and we returned to school, disappointed that the Americans weren't pressing the attack. After what seemed like an interminable time, the planes finally returned on October 15, and there were several more days of raids. Then again everything went quiet, and we wondered what was happening until November 5, when the raids resumed. Now we knew for sure that something was going on somewhere in the Philippines, and the increasing nastiness of the Japanese assured us that what ever it was, it wasn't good for them.

FIFTEEN

AMERICAN FORCES ON THE MOVE

In the autumn of 1944, we had no way of knowing the American strategic situation in the Pacific. After a slow start following the attack on Pearl Harbor, American forces had achieved a string of victories over the past two years, bringing them ever closer to the inner defense line for the Japanese Empire. Admiral Chester W. Nimitz's Pacific Fleet had island-hopped through the Gilberts, Marshalls, Carolines, Marianas, and Palaus. With the construction of airfields in the Marianas, the Army Air Force was within striking distance of the Japanese Home Islands using its new B-29 Super Fortresses. To the south, General MacArthur, had captured the Solomons and New Guinea.

The American Joint Chiefs of Staff had discussed what the next objective should be. One line of thought recommended taking Formosa, which would put the American forces right on the doorstep of the Japanese Home Islands and be an excellent jumping off point for their invasion. However, this strategy was mitigated by the fact that the Chinese armies on the mainland were making little progress against the Japanese to clear the coast of China for such an invasion. General MacArthur argued for an invasion of the Philippines, which would block Japan from its essential resources in the East Indies and Malaya. MacArthur's recommendation prevailed, and the decision was made to invade the Philippines during the autumn of 1944.

The largest concentration of Japanese forces outside of China and the Home Islands were in the Philippines. Further, American intelligence indicated that the Japanese were reinforcing their ground forces in the islands, so an early invasion was essential. Initially, the plan was to invade both Mindanao and Leyte, but air strikes in the Philippines during September and October were so successful that strategists decided to concentrate on Leyte alone, and plans were made for an invasion on October 20. Meanwhile, the Japanese were convinced that by reinforcing the islands, they could defeat the Americans wherever they landed in the Philippines.

To take Leyte, the Americans mounted the largest amphibious operation to date in the Pacific. The landing was successful, but then encountered fierce resistance as the troops moved inland. Japanese bombers from Luzon and other islands attacked the land forces, while the Seventh Fleet provided air cover. Then at the end of October, the Japanese unleashed their most fearsome new weapon—Kamikaze suicide bombers. Flying from airstrips around Clark Field north of Manila, Kamikazes badly punished the American invasion fleet.

Then Japan committed almost its entire remaining fleet to destroying the American invasion fleet in the largest naval engagement of World War II, the Battle of Leyte Gulf. They came very close to success when Admiral Halsey's main fleet was lured away by a Japanese decoy fleet. However, the heroic efforts of the light American escort carriers were able to stave off the main Japanese assault fleet, turning it back before it could devastate the helpless American landing task force at Leyte. The battle decimated the Japanese fleets, which were unable for the remainder of the war to mount another meaningful operation.

Misreading the results of the naval battle, the Japanese command committed reinforcements to their troops on Leyte, drawing out the battle for many days. Although the fighting lasted into May of 1945, organized Japanese resistance ended by December 31, 1944. The Battle of Leyte Gulf cost the Japanese enormously in men and materiel. Now American forces were ready to move on to their main objective, capturing the island of Luzon and the Philippine capital of Manila, where the majority of the Japanese land forces remained.

∞ ∞ ∞

In Santo Tomas, we were isolated from any news of the war. Yet, the news of the Leyte landings somehow reached leaders in our camp administration. It wasn't until after the war that we discovered the carefully kept secret. Interned with us were a number of radio engineers who had smuggled components into camp and built two radio receivers and two transmitters. The components were distributed among several people who hid them from the frequent searches the Japanese made of people's belongings. Had the Japanese found any of these components, they would have executed the people who had them.

When a movie screen was erected in the plaza in 1942, the engineers secretly built an antenna into the structure. Now the engineers could assemble their radio and receive and send messages on the short wave band. The radio primarily was used for receiving messages, which could not be detected by the Japanese, but the capability to send was available in case of an emergency. The Japanese suspected that such a radio existed, but with numerous searches, were unable to find it or any of its components.

At the end of October of 1944, a routine announcement was made over the camp PA system. Announcements were made frequently to advise people of changes of regulations and other administrative topics. I always listened to them because they might include something important like the change in meal times. The subject of this particular announcement was fairly innocuous, something about people having to turn some kind of information in to the administration by a certain deadline. It ended with the cutesy phrase, "Better latey than never". It was a coded message that a few people picked up, substituting Leyte for latey. Immediately the interpretation spread through camp, and we were all elated that the Americans had landed on Leyte, an island less than 300 miles to the southwest of Manila.

∞ ∞ ∞

One of our intellectual games was to use Western customs, euphemisms, and double entendres to fool the Japanese. It was one of the things that contributed to keeping our morale from completely disintegrating along with our lives. One of the best morale boosters was a large cartoon poster an artist drew and posted in the rear lobby of the Main Building. A new one was posted about once a month, and I always looked forward to seeing what kind of private jab the artist was conveying.

I remember one that showed a man with his food bowl and a caption that announced that it was a good thing that he had a cast iron stomach. From that time on, I would look reflectively at my stomach to discern how it had hardened to be able to digest the slop we had for food.

Another poster showed a group of women around a table with baskets of rice. The caption was, "D-light in, D-bugging, D-rice". This of course referred to the poor quality of staples that the Japanese were supplying, filled with weevils and other contaminants.

At Thanksgiving, a poster appeared which was split. On the left, captioned 1941, a fat man sat at a table burdened with food. Adjacent to it on the right, captioned 1944, sat an emaciated man with a little slop on his plate. Underneath was a poem. "Tis easy to be pleasant, when life goes by like a song. . . . But the man worth while, is the man who can smile, when everything goes all wrong."

And probably my favorite was a picture of a graduating student reading a letter he is writing. "Dear Uncle—This is an urgent invitation to attend my graduation! Only your presence can make this great experience of my life a complete success. Affectionately, Joe Internee." This, of course, was a plea for Uncle Sam to liberate us.

∞ ∞ ∞

After the end of October, air raids came in rapid succession. We were confident the Americans knew where we were, and so became quite casual about where we sheltered. Initially, my mother believed we needed to be in the concrete Main Building for protection. But after awhile, we became more confident, and when the air raid alert sounded, would save the energy of walking from our shanty all the way to the Main Building by just ducking into the nearby Annex. Some people dug air raid shelters next to their shanties, as did our neighbors the Honors, who dug out a pit under their floor. I pitched in, helping to dig, and on several occasions took advantage of its proximity to duck into it and avoid having to leave our shanty area.

School was suspended, and by January the air-raid alert was constant with no all-clear signal, so we totally ignored the concept of shelter and just lived our lives as best we could because the bombers could be overhead at any time of day or night. Despite our relaxed attitude towards air raids, the Japanese still tried to maintain discipline and punished anyone they caught looking up into the sky. The punishment was to make the culprit stand unprotected staring into the sun for several hours. In one case, a person being punished was badly injured when hit in the head by shrapnel. I was always very careful about where and when I took a peek at the attacking aircraft.

The falling shrapnel now produced a new activity for us kids. After each raid, we would spread out across the campus and search for pieces to add to our collection or to trade with others, like baseball cards. Pieces as small as one-quarter inch were valued. I spent hours searching the ground for the jagged pieces and trying to dig bullets from dogfights out of the ground. Eventually, I accumulated six pieces of shrapnel for my collection, none of them more than an inch across. When we sheltered in the Annex, we'd hear the clang of falling shrapnel as it hit the galvanized iron of the roof, and I just knew that, if I could figure out how to get up to the roof, I'd greatly enhance my collection. On one occasion, we returned to our shanty after a raid and found a jagged hole clear through our cupboard, which sent me into a frantic, but unsuccessful, search for the piece of shrapnel that had made it.

One day in December, I was sheltering in the Honor's bomb shelter during an air raid. The heavy rumbling of engines overhead led us to leave the shelter and see what the cause of the noise was. Passing over us were several formations of four-engine bombers with fighter aircraft surrounding them. Looking at my reference book, I discovered that the bombers were beautiful silver B-29 Superfortresses, the biggest aircraft in the American arsenal and only experimental before the war. The fighters were twin-boomed P-38 Lightenings. We danced all around and shouted our greetings to these first land-based aircraft to join the bombing raids, briefly not caring whether the Japanese saw us.

As the big bombers came more frequently, we noticed that the Japanese anti-aircraft fire seemed to trail the formations. One of the men grinned, and commented that the Japanese didn't seem to have any concept of Kentucky windage and didn't lead the aircraft when aiming their guns. Anything that showed how the Americans outclassed the Japanese made us very happy. Then one day in January, the anti-aircraft guns got lucky and hit one of the bombers. I was shocked to see the airplane explode, then counted the number of parachutes that opened, and grieved because I knew that there were fewer parachutes than the number of crew on the big plane.

With the big bombers, we noticed much more damage being done in and around the city. The bombing resulted in a very satisfying rolling thunder as the sticks of bombs exploded in succession, and sometimes I would hear a secondary explosion, which meant something important had been hit. After each raid, I would notice large fires around us on different sides of the city, depending on the objective of the raid.

∞ ∞ ∞

With the bombings, the Japanese became increasingly belligerent. They increased the frequency of their searches of the shanty areas and the dormitories in the various buildings. Anything they declared as illegal, which included a variety of things from electrical appliances to notebooks, was confiscated and the owner arbitrarily sentenced to several days of hard time in their jail, which was located in the Education Building.

Rations were cut further, and, as an early Christmas present on December 23, the Japanese reduced our meal schedule to two meals a day. Breakfast at 8:30 consisted of a thin porridge called lugao; dinner at 4:00 consisted of a watery soup with greens from the garden plots and a few beans. That left a long seven and one-half hours with nothing to put into our stomachs.

Roll calls were held twice a day, once at 9:00 and again at 5:30. These assemblies, where we had to stand in the hall and wait for the Japanese guards to come and take our count, were often prolonged, sometimes leaving us standing in the hallways for hours at a time. Curfew was at 7:00 in the evening, after which we were not allowed out of our building, and lights-out was at 8:00. That made for a long night lying on my hard wooden pallet, but it really didn't bother me since I didn't have much energy to spare being restless. The long nights helped the days to pass faster, though those waits between meals seemed interminable.

Christmas of 1944 did not have the spirit of the previous two. We no longer had the physical or mental resources to make it a special occasion. But we were grateful that our camp leaders recognized the holiday by making a special distribution of food that exhausted the last of the camp's reserves which had been held back for emergencies. Our Christmas dinner quantity was increased by twenty percent, and I was given a bonanza of one teaspoon of jam and a one-half ounce piece of chocolate, which fed a sweet tooth that hadn't tasted anything sugary for so long that I couldn't remember the last time.

Christmas Evening, after roll call, a bunch of us, including adults and kids, were sitting at a table in the hallway outside of our dorm, as we often did in the evening before lights-out. We were talking about some of the great Christmas celebrations we'd had in the past, when the conversation reverted to our favorite subject—food. Each of us described the Christmas feast we would have after we were liberated. Each person lovingly described his or her fantasy—roast goose, turkey with all the trimmings, baked ham, and so on. Our stomachs rumbled and grumbled in complaint from the watery soup with a few greens and beans that had been our fare that afternoon, nowhere close to our dream meals. Then came the turn of a boy about six years old, who wasn't old enough to remember a Christmas before we were interned. The statement of his ideal Christmas meal was short and succinct, "I'm gonna have beans!" The thought of a nice plate of boiled beans made my mouth water more than the thought of goose and roast potatoes because it was so much closer to the reality we were living.

New Year's Eve arrived, but it had little meaning to us. We were locked down at eight in the evening with the lights turned out. Across the way in the Education Building, we could hear the shouts and laughter of our carousing Japanese guards, who were partying like there was no tomorrow. In truth, that may have been the case because their world was nearing its end.

SIXTEEN

THE RACE TO MANILA

January 1945 marked the beginning of my fourth year in Santo Tomas. No longer was internment the lark that I thought it was at the beginning. Starvation steadily dragged us down. My mother weighed about 130 pounds before we entered Santo Tomas. She now weighed 85 to 90 pounds. Before the war, she was a strong, athletic woman, but now was reduced to arms and legs like toothpicks with bones showing prominently every-where. She was barely able to drag herself around. When we left China, I weighed 52 pounds. Although 3-inches taller now, I still weighed 50 pounds. My sister and I were in much better shape than our mother, or, for that matter, most of the adults in the camp. We benefited greatly from better treatment, not to mention the sacrifices our mother made to protect us.

During the previous December, one percent of our fellow prisoners died. In January, an even higher percentage passed on. The Japanese Commandant called our head doctor to his office, pointed to the death certificates our doctors had filled out, and demanded to know why the cause of death in each case said either malnutrition or starvation. The doctor carefully explained that the prisoners were simply not receiving enough food. In some cases, beriberi led to organ failures that caused death. In other cases, victims simply died from starvation.

The Commandant rejected the doctor's explanation. The prisoners, the Commandant said, were getting just as much food as the Japanese garrison. This was a blatant lie. In fact, the Japanese had been taking food from the stores for the prisoners and eating it themselves. When the Commandant demanded the doctor revise the death certificates, the doctor refused. He was dismissed and shortly afterwards was thrown into the Japanese jail. The Japanese released him after a few days.

Families were now reduced to making grim decisions—would one of the adults sacrifice by giving his or her ration to the other parent and children? Which parent could best raise the children if one had to die? Were there other alternatives to end this misery?

∞ ∞ ∞

As January wore down towards February, smaller B-26 twin-engine bombers replaced the great waves of B-29s. They swept in low over the city with chattering machine guns. Soon P-51 and P-47 fighter aircraft joined them, flying even closer to bomb and strafe targets right next to the prison walls. Those who knew airplanes said these were short-range aircraft, which could only mean that the Americans were close. Japanese resistance against the raids seemed non-existent, and the attacks took an ever-increasing toll on their resources. Certainly less food was available to the now clearly starving prisoners.

Although we knew American forces were close, we had no idea where or how close they were. One clue, however—the Japanese garrison became increasingly belligerent. We had to stand for roll calls that sometimes lasted hours. They arrested four camp leaders on vague charges and took them to Fort Santiago and a visit with the Kempetai, the Japanese secret police. The four men were never again seen alive. A few weeks later, their bodies were found in a shallow grave in one of Manila's parks, along with Filipinos who had been chained together and shot.

My mother's thriftiness in saving food from our comfort kits and making hardtack served us well. We were desperately hungry and weak, but not yet in immediate danger from the effects of beriberi or direct starvation. But with the recent reduction in meals, her hoard was now rapidly disappearing. Soon nothing would be left to supplement our pitiful twice-daily ration. In reality, we were in a grim race with death. Or, for some, perhaps liberation would win.

∞ ∞ ∞

Japanese General Yamashita led the more than a quarter-million troops entrenched on Luzon. Although he knew he could not defeat the fresher and better-equipped American force, Yamashita was determined to delay the Allies' march towards the Japanese home islands. He concentrated his troops in three groups in the Central Cordillera, leaving only 10,000 troops in Manila, which he believed was indefensible. He ordered them to destroy all of the bridges and strategic installations, then to evacuate the city when the Americans arrived.

Japanese Admiral Iwabachi, also in Manila, commanded 16,000 troops of the Manila Naval Defense Force. Although nominally under the command of General Yamashita, the Admiral countermanded the General's order and placed the army troops under his own command. This well-armed and entrenched force prepared to defend the city rather than to evacuate it.

As the Japanese resistance on Leyte diminished, MacArthur turned his attention to the island of Mindoro. American troops landed on December 15, 1944, and within a few days set up airfields that could support landings on Luzon and directly attack airbases from which Kamikazes were flying.

On January 9, 1945, American forces came ashore a little over 100 miles north of Manila at Lingayen Gulf. MacArthur's advanced troops immediately pressed south across the central Luzon plain towards Manila. The forces encountered little resistance until January 23 when they reached Clark Field, about half way to Manila, where they faced one of Yamashita's defensive forces. Fierce fighting delayed the advance until the end of January. Another landing, at Subic Bay on January 29, cut off Japanese access to Bataan. On January 31, in a plan to recapture the southern end of the island, forces landed 45 miles southwest of Manila. MacArthur, however, changed this force's mission and ordered it to immediately drive on Manila from the south.

The Americans had broken the Japanese code. A message from Tokyo to field commanders in the Philippines said, "Kill all military and civilian prisoners before the Americans can liberate them." Then the American Army received a message from a secret transmitter in the Santo Tomas Internment Camp that said, "The Japanese appear to be preparing to execute the prisoners in the camp."

Unhappy with the pace and the aggressiveness of the main invasion force led by the 37th Infantry, MacArthur met with General Mudge, Commander of the newly arrived 1st Cavalry Division. He told him, "Go to Manila, go around the Nips, bounce off the Nips, but go to Manila. Rescue the prisoners at Santo Tomas." The general set up a flying column to lead the race to Manila across the central plain of Luzon while the 37th Infantry pressed forward along the coast.

Between the jumping-off point for the flying column and Manila sat the infamous Cabanatuan POW camp. The general feared that the flying column could not reach the camp to free the prisoners before the Japanese executed them. MacArthur authorized a special mission. On the night of January 30, the 6th Ranger Battalion slipped through the Japanese lines, and, in a daring raid with the help of Filipino guerillas, caught the Japanese by surprise and rescued 513 prisoners. They were the remaining survivors of Bataan and Corregidor who were too weak to ship to Japan or Manchuria as slave laborers.

At one minute after midnight on February 1, after the rescued POWs were safely inside American lines, the 800-man 44th Tank Battalion, spearheading the flying column, broke through the Japanese lines. By morning it had reached Cabanatuan and rolled right on through, racing down the main highway. A Marine fighter wing flying SBD Douglas Dauntless dive bombers provided close air support.

The battalion raced south, encountered stiff resistance, cut through it, zigged and zagged to cross rivers and go around fortifications, sometimes moving as fast as 50 m.p.h on the main highway, other times almost crawling backwards as they sought a way to cross another river. On the evening of February 2, with Manila almost within view, the tanks and vehicles ran out of fuel. They had moved so fast that they had outrun their supply column. That night they bivouacked with barely enough fuel for the tanks in their perimeter guard. But fuel trucks arrived the next morning, and they pressed on to Manila. Japanese units, leaving Manila to join Yamashita's forces in the mountains, were surprised to encounter American troops so near the city and were easily over run.

Late in the afternoon of February 3, the flying column reached the outskirts of the city. A Filipino guerilla unit joined up with the column and, as it led the way into the city, avoided Japanese defenses. At about 8:30 that evening, the first squadron of cavalry arrived at the Calle España entrance to Santo Tomas. Now they faced a dilemma. The arching iron of the gate was too low for the tanks to pass through. The commanding officers of the cavalry and the guerilla unit dismounted from their jeep and examined the situation, to decide how they would bring the column into the campus. A Japanese guard tossed a hand grenade at the two officers. The American commander was wounded and the Filipino, Captain Colayco, received numerous grenade fragments in his abdomen.

Corpsmen carried the men to the boulevard's center divider, where they could be protected from enemy fire. Mortally wounded, Captain Colayco soon died. Meanwhile, the column of tanks, trucks, and jeeps with engines running, extended behind them along Calle España, an isolated force of a few hundred men surrounded by 26,000 defenders.

∞ ∞ ∞

February 3, 1945, started out pretty much like a normal Saturday, given the conditions in which we lived. I went down to the Annex to get my breakfast of watery lugao gruel and then returned to our dormitory for morning roll call. Today the roll call went quickly, without the long delays we came to expect. I then went out to our shanty with my mother and sister. It was a beautiful morning, clear and warm, but not too hot. A sense of anticipation hung in the air. Everyone was smiling for a change. There was no real reason to expect something special, but "something" was there, and the anticipation continued to build all day.

A little after mid morning, I heard the far off whine of an airplane flying very low in our direction. By now, I had become quite expert at understanding the sounds that various aircraft made and could usually anticipate their missions. But this sound was different. I raced out of the shanty and stared in the direction of the sound.

A low-flying fighter approached from the north. The roar increased as it whizzed by almost directly overhead at perhaps 100 feet. As I stared upward, I could see the gunner in the rear cockpit of an SBD dive-bomber wave. What excitement I felt! Now, this was no ordinary day.

Soon, word spread throughout the camp that the gunner had dropped his goggles with a note into one of the courtyards of the Main Building. It read, "Roll out the barrel." For us, this was rife with meaning because it was from the words of a song that ends, "for the gang's all here." I later learned that the full text of the message read, "Roll out the barrel, Santa Claus is coming to town Sunday or Monday." This meant that we would be rescued in only one or two more days. A long time later, I also learned that the gunner had a brother in Santo Tomas and was anxious to get a message of hope to all of us.

That afternoon, two more low-flying SBDs passed from west to east, the pilots and gunners waving as they zoomed by. The sense of anticipation I felt earlier in the day increased, becoming an almost painful feeling in my chest.

At dinnertime, I went to the Annex and collected my bowl of pitiful "stew" and took it back to our shanty to eat with my mother and sister. After dinner, we returned to the dormitory for evening roll call. Again it was taken without delay. If anything unusual was happening outside our walls or at the guards' head-quarters in the Education Building, the demeanor of the guards taking roll call didn't give any clue.

After being dismissed, with about an hour before curfew, I went to the ground floor of the Main Building to the shower room to clean up and brush my teeth before bed. I went out of the rear entrance to the building into the balmy evening air. It was twilight, the sun set, but still not dark with a pinkish orange glow in the sky. Smoke rose from various directions around us, and there were occasional explosions in the distance.

As the sky darkened, flares frequently lit up the sky. That in itself was unusual and notable. What really caught my attention was a barely discernible very low-pitched constant rumble that I seemed to feel in my body rather than hear. My friends and I were just awed by the spectacle. Then one of them whispered, "Maybe it's the Japanese coming to kill us." A shiver ran up my spine, but rationalization calmed the momentary apprehension. Why would the Japanese bring in troops from elsewhere to kill us? Lieutenant Colonel Hayashi, the camp commander, and his second in command, Lt. Abiko, had a large enough garrison to do it themselves. Time and again they had demonstrated the cruelty to be capable of such an act.

I lingered as long as I could before returning to the building because of curfew, while both of these phenomena continued, even increasing in intensity. The anticipation that had been building all day reached a new peak. I could feel tenseness in my chest and stomach, like the feeling I got in later years when I was about to make a presentation to a large audience. This stage fright was a combination of anxiety and anticipation, and yes, very definitely excitement.

I returned to the third floor of the building. My mother and sister were sitting in the hallway outside our dormitory at a card table, as we usually did between curfew and lights out. I was so excited to tell them about what I had seen and heard outside that I hardly noticed that they were excited too. My mother then brought out her precious tin box and opened it to reveal that only two of the hardtack biscuits that were sustaining our lives remained. She took one out and carefully broke it into three equal pieces, and we each nibbled on our share. It wasn't enough to stave off the hunger, but it is all we ever got. Then she did something very out of character for this careful, thrifty lady. She reached in and took out the last biscuit and shared it also, saying, "What the heck, this will all be over very soon anyway." She did mean that we'd be rescued in the next two or three days didn't she?

What I didn't know then was that the Japanese, following orders from Tokyo, were beginning the destruction of Manila. The Japanese were very disciplined, believing that all orders came directly from their Emperor through the people who commanded them. They greatly revered their Emperor and would do anything he wanted. Would they now also follow the orders from Tokyo and kill us all?

SEVENTEEN

LIBERATION!

The American column could not remain strung out along España Street in such an indefensible position. So Captain Jesse Walters in the lead tank, "Battlin' Basic," lined it up perpendicular to the wall and battered through the wall and fence adjacent to the gate. He then proceeded into Santo Tomas, followed by the rest of the column.

The tanks, with searchlights on and accompanied by infantry, slowly advanced along the entry street towards the plaza. The Japanese garrison, after desultory defensive fire, fled to the Education Building and blockaded themselves inside. They had an excellent defensive position in the concrete building and held 218 prisoners as hostages on the third floor.

Lieutenant Abiko, second in command and subordinate to Lieutenant Colonel Hayashi, both much hated by the prisoners because of our cruel and inhumane treatment, tried to rally his troops. He emerged from the guardhouse at the end of the Education Building with a grenade to attack the Americans. He was quickly shot down. The tank column was now unimpeded as it entered the plaza in front of the Main Building.

∞ ∞ ∞

We sat at our table in the hallway outside of our third floor dormitory savoring the last crumbs of our hardtack in the minutes before lights-out. Then, indistinctive in the distance, we heard the rumble of a myriad of voices screaming. The excitement was clear but the words were not recognizable at first, swelling and becoming clearer as the sound flowed up the stairways and along the hallways like a flood as successive groups of people picked up the scream. The message was relayed from person to person, repeated over and over again until we could clearly hear it. "They're here, They're here!"

When I finally understood, I jumped to my feet and started screaming myself as I raced along the hallway towards the main staircase. Reaching it, I almost tumbled down the stairs in my haste to get to the second floor, then down to the lobby on the main floor. But when I reached the mezzanine, the crowd was backed up the stairs, and I could go no further. I stood on the mezzanine landing and looked down into the main lobby. What I saw gave my heart another jolt. I was already running on adrenaline, my breath panting from the run, and the sight almost overwhelmed me.

The large double doors from the lobby to the plaza were pushed open, and the front end of a tank stuck through it, its main gun pointed in my direction. Around it, jumping and screaming, were fellow prisoners, throwing their arms around a group of soldiers and kissing them. The GIs just stood around with big silly grins on their faces.

In the lobby just to the side of the main entrance, a Japanese soldier was lying on the ground. American soldiers stood around him. I asked what had happened. Someone in front of me said that the Japanese soldier had attacked the Americans with a grenade and had been shot. He looked pretty dead to me, but this incident led to one of the great controversies of our liberation.

In years to come, the legend developed that after Lieutenant Abiko was shot, he was then brought into the Main Building. There, he was taken into the clinic just off the lobby by a group of liberated prisoners, who proceeded to cut his throat and kill him. They then dragged his body to the rear lobby and posed it with his feet pointed towards Tokyo, which was considered a great insult to the Emperor.

Whether these prisoners committed murder after their liberation is the question. Some contemporary historians claim this was a rumor, but the act never happened. Others I have talked to claim they saw Abiko's body under the stairwell in the rear lobby. I used the same stairwell numerous times the next day and never saw a body. Furthermore, the Army immediately occupied the clinic where the murder allegedly happened. It had become an aid station and surgery room for the men wounded at the gate and in the continuing fighting on the campus. There was little opportunity for the extra-curricula activity claimed. One of the Filipino guerillas came forward to say that he was the one who shot Abiko as he emerged from the guard station with the hand grenade, but no one admitted to being a member of the lynch mob.

My theory is that Abiko died from the gunshot wound, probably in the lobby of the Main Building. The prisoners then dragged his body to the rear lobby where they posed him, and his body was removed early the next day. The report of the murder then was fabricated because of the anger we held for this horrible man. After all, he had been responsible, at least partially, for the murder of four of our leaders just within the past couple of weeks.

∞ ∞ ∞

As I stood on the Mezzanine landing looking down into the lobby, the tank backed out from the large door, and soldiers started herding people into the building from the plaza. I could hear small-arms firing outside and wondered where the fighting was going on. One of the people who had been in the plaza told me the Japanese were shooting at people in the plaza.

It seemed like the celebration in the lobby was over, and all but a few of the American troops had dispersed. I started to climb the stairs back up to my dormitory when a squad of troops came running up the stairs calling, "Gangway, gangway," and passed me carrying their rifles, two machine guns, and boxes of ammunition. I followed them to the third floor, but when they continued on up to the roof, I turned towards my dormitory. Looking from the dormitory window, I had a panoramic view of the Education Building and the road and field in front of it.

Chaos reined. Four tanks, drawn up about 100 feet in front of the Education Building with soldiers crouching behind and between them, raked the building with machine gun fire. Soldiers fired rifles and machine guns into the building as well. The Japanese returned fire, and the night was lit up by tracer bullets flying in both directions.

Then the two machine guns that had just been carried to the roof of my building opened up, providing enfilade fire down the hallways of the Education Building. They were located right above my dormitory, probably not more than ten feet above my head. I could follow the tracers as they raced across the street and through the windows of the building opposite. The fierce firefight continued for about 20 minutes and then started to diminish. The Japanese were taking casualties from the crossfire, so they went to the third floor and dispersed among the hostages. Every once in awhile, one of them would sneak over to a window and snipe at the American troops, which would elicit an overwhelming return fire. After a time, the Japanese realized this was unproductive, and just laid low.

The Americans also took casualties in the fighting. Wounded men were brought into the clinic in the Main Building where the Army doctor and corpsmen, assisted by our own just-freed doctors and Army and Navy nurses, worked on them all night.

When the fighting drew to a stalemate and the shooting stopped, I climbed onto my cot and immediately fell fast asleep, the tension and excitement of the day finally catching up with me. Sporadic firing was still being heard outside of the walls. One troop of cavalry was diverted to capture the Malacañang Palace, which was the official home of the President of the Philippines during peacetime. The last troop in the flying column got lost after entering Manila and entered Santo Tomas sometime later during the night. Overnight, Santo Tomas became an armed camp. Tank commanders took defensive positions while infantry dug in to defend against a Japanese counterattack. During this time, I was sound asleep and heard none of the activity.

∞ ∞ ∞

In the morning, I went to the Annex for a breakfast of the same mush we had been eating, except this morning it was thick instead of the usual watery gruel. The kitchen was anticipating a new supply of food from the army. The cooks prepared the last of the cereal in our storeroom, and as poor as the meal might have been in ordinary times, it was a very satisfying way to celebrate our first morning of liberation.

From breakfast, I went straight out to our shanty. No need to return to the dorm for the hated roll call. Not far from the front of our shanty, two troopers had dug foxholes and pointed their machine gun towards the wall. Their foxholes were not deep because the water table was only about three-feet down. They were long and shallow, with a berm around the head end where the machine gun was set up. The troopers lay in the foxholes and scanned along the wall.

I sat next to their foxholes, and we started to chat. They seemed happy to have someone to talk with, answered my many questions, and soon explained how their water-cooled machine gun operated. After awhile, one of them rummaged in his pack and pulled out a candy bar. He looked over at me and said that they had been instructed not to give food to any of the prisoners since it could make us sick. But he slipped it to me anyway, telling me to be careful how I ate it. Soon a crowd of other people had gathered, and I slipped away to enjoy the first candy bar I had in more than three years. I wondered how those soldiers could attend to their guard duty with so many excited people gathered around them.

Wonder of wonders, the kitchen served lunch today. Although it was still the same "stew" we had been served, now lots more beans filled the bowl. More than six weeks had passed since we last had been served lunch. At this point, our kitchen was still using the supplies from our own storage because the Cavalry was traveling light and did not bring surplus food. The troopers "dined" on individual packages of C-rations with their small cans of meat, dried fruit, and powdered coffee and milk. This was a high-protein diet, and the doctors warned that the prisoners would have to be eased into a richer diet or we would all become sick.

The standoff between the Japanese in the Education Building and the surrounding American troops continued, but negotiations had been initiated to grant the Japanese freedom in exchange for freeing the hostages. As a sign of goodwill, the guards allowed a hot meal to be brought into their fortress for themselves and their hostages. Later, when I talked with people who had been hostages, they said that the tense situation became more relaxed. They now had freedom to roam around the third floor, though they were not allowed to get to the stairwells. Some even were able to lean out of the windows and talk to the tank crews.

Additional units of the 1st Cavalry arrived. I walked around the Main Building to the plaza, using the road between it and the seminary rather than the one I usually used next to the Education Building because of the Japanese defending it. The plaza was packed with military vehicles. Tanks lined the southern edge next to the grove of trees. Trucks and jeeps filled a lot of the space between the tanks and the Main Building. Tanks and soldiers were still lined up facing the front of the Education Building, and no doubt were also lined up along the back, but all was quiet inside.

As I walked along the line of tanks, a trooper sitting on the back of one called to me. "Hey kid, you want some lemonade?" I wasn't about to turn that down, and drank greedily from his canteen cup.

The 1st Cavalry was a battle-hardened unit, fresh from the fighting in Leyte, and weary from the race to Manila. The kids in Santo Tomas must have touched their hearts, skinny bodies in ragged clothes, practically naked, and ribs prominent in our bare chests, but ever cheerful. The soldiers weren't about to obey some stupid rule about not giving us treats. And it took damned little to make us happy!

The adults were an even more pitiful sight, especially the men whose ration was no larger than the rest of us, but had to fill their bigger frames and fuel their harder work. They dressed much like the kids, just shorts, though they tended to wear dis-integrating sandals, many of them home made. In this uniform, their arms and legs were like pipe cleaners, their chests hollow, and ribs prominent. A six-foot tall man probably weighed less than 100 pounds. I think the troopers felt very proud that they had liberated us, and now wondered what they could do to make our lives easier. What they didn't realize was that we had adapted to a simpler life than they could ever imagine, and for the moment, just being out from under the cruel heel of the Japanese was plenty for us.

∞ ∞ ∞

All was quiet in the Education Building, and the American Army was occupying North Manila with a minimum of resistance. The Japanese did not counterattack on our little fortress, and only occasionally did we hear bursts of small-arms fire outside the walls. The GIs started to relax.

Confined within the walls of Santo Tomas, the American troops now needed to determine the disposition of the Japanese defenders. Diosdado Guaytingco, who had accompanied the guerillas into the camp and stayed with Captain Colayco until he died of his wounds, offered to retrieve the records about the Japanese defenses that he had compiled as an intelligence agent. The commanding general offered to send a squad of soldiers to protect him, but he refused the offer, saying that it was too dangerous with Japanese soldiers spread throughout the city. Instead, he climbed over the wall near the gymnasium and set out alone to recover his documents and return with them to Santo Tomas.

The Army also dispatched tank and foot patrols around the immediate area of the campus. That evening, a foot patrol was cautiously proceeding down a street a few hundred yards west of Santo Tomas. On one side of the street were buildings and on the other was a high wall. As they called to each other to keep in contact in the gathering gloom, they heard a voice from the other side of the wall. "Hey, are you Americans?" They replied that they were, and the voice continued. "Can you get us out of here? We're POWs."

The patrol had stumbled on Bilibid prison, a place the army was not even aware existed. The Spanish had built the stark gray mass in the 1800s as a high-security prison, and it had become a federal penitentiary when the Americans took over the Philippines in 1898. Because it was inhumane by modern standards, the Americans had built a new federal penitentiary at Multinlupa, south of Manila, essentially abandoning the old hulk. When the Japanese arrived, they reactivated Bilibid, using it as a waypoint for the transfer of POWs. In the early part of the war, prisoners from Corregidor and other parts of the island were imprisoned there before being transferred to Camp O'Donnell and Cabanatuan POW camps. Later, the POWs assigned to work as slave laborers were temporarily imprisoned in Bilibid before being transferred to the "Hell Ships" docked in Manila Bay that would take them on the hazardous voyages to Japan and Manchuria.

In Bilibid that evening were 800 POWs plus 550 civilian prisoners recently transferred from Baguio up in the mountains where General Yamashita was preparing to make his last stand. The patrol was not in a position to handle the number of prisoners, so they informed them they would be back in the morning with reinforcements. As it turned out, the 37th Infantry arrived in Manila the next day, having taken a different route than the 1st Cavalry, and they were the ones to free the prisoners. With the city still under Japanese control, Bilibid was located in an untenable position to defend and support 1,350 freed prisoners, so most of them were moved to a factory located away from where fierce fighting was about to erupt. Others who were too weak to remain were moved to Santo Tomas, and then air evacuated to Mindoro, where they were placed on transports and hospital ships for the voyage home.

∞ ∞ ∞

On the morning of February 5, almost two days after the Japanese had taken their hostages in the Education Building, the negotiations reached a satisfactory conclusion. In exchange for freeing the hostages, the Japanese soldiers would be allowed to retain their weapons and would be released beyond the American lines into a neighborhood specifically designated by the Japanese. Late in the morning, 70 surviving guards emerged from the Education Building under the leadership of Lieutenant Colonel Hiyashi. They carried their weapons and their wounded as they marched out of camp. The ex-prisoners cheered as they watched them go.

The hostages were free, and it was time to count the casualties. Amazingly, the heavy hail of fire into the building resulted in few casualties among the civilians. Most wounds were abrasions and bruises resulting from flying chunks of concrete and ricocheting bullets. One man had died of a heart attack, and he could be considered the first death directly due to enemy action.

Unknown to the Japanese during their negotiations was that they had chosen to be released in an area where a Filipino guerilla unit was operating. The Americans notified the unit of the impending release, and the Filipinos arranged an appropriate reception. The English might have said that what the Americans did wasn't cricket, but who the hell cared. To the liberated prisoners' way of thinking, the cruel, murdering bastards deserved whatever they got!

Shortly after they were released, the Filipinos engaged them in a fierce firefight, killing all but a handful. The survivors were brought back into Santo Tomas in the afternoon and placed in the shed located between the Annex and the Infirmary that had been used for grinding coconuts. Shortly afterwards, I joined a group of other kids who were standing around the shed staring at the prisoners. The once-proud guards sat on the bare ground with their hands tied behind their backs, heads bowed, looking very dejected. Then one of the kids shouted, "One, two, three, bow," and we all bowed just as we had been trained to do in respect for the Japanese. Then we all burst into laughter and hooted and jeered at the prisoners. The tables had finally turned.

∞ ∞ ∞

At the time, I gave little thought to why the Cavalry arrived in Santo Tomas so unexpectedly. Prodded by General MacArthur and moving faster than anyone could believe possible, they had covered 100 miles from their breakout point, facing heavy resistance at times, in just under three days. I was just so happy to finally be liberated that it didn't occur to me that they had achieved what came to be known as, "One of the most dramatic rescues in the history of warfare".

When the hostages were freed, the prisoners celebrated by raising an American flag that had been smuggled into Santo Tomas and kept hidden from the Japanese until this momentous moment. (Photo courtesy of the American Historical collection, Ateneo de Manila University.)

*When liberated, the prisoners in Santo Tomas were
starving, as illustrated by these two newly rescued
men. (Photo courtesy of the American Historical
Collection, Atneo de Manila University.)*

Later, after I had moved to America and entered high school,
I enrolled in an American History class. On the first day, we
were handed our textbooks, and I went straight home after
school and cracked mine open to the chapter on World War II. I
was particularly interested in this chapter because I had missed
the day-to-day news reports from the battlefronts and knew little
of how the war had progressed. I was anxious to learn what the
American strategy was and how it was carried out.

The chapter was somewhere between 20 and 30 pages long,
and was a very succinct compilation of three and one-half years
of the American war effort. It certainly wasn't enough to get into
any detail, and I was rather disappointed. As I neared the end of

the chapter, I came across a short paragraph. It mentioned the liberation of Santo Tomas. For the first time, I saw in print that the race to Manila by the 1st Cavalry had been in response to a radio signal from within the camp warning of the impending execution of all of the prisoners by the Japanese.

In the years that have passed since then, historians have attributed the rescue of the prisoners in Santo Tomas to all kinds of different motivations. The subject has been dissolved, crystallized, and reconstituted with an excess of analysis and a dearth of clarity. No history that I have seen has ever duplicated the brief and succinct explanation written by the author of that textbook so shortly after the event happened.

∞ ∞ ∞

Although we continued to hear bursts of small-arms fire, the Americans didn't seem to be meeting much resistance as they started to occupy Manila. General MacArthur believed that Manila would quickly be pacified and occupied, and his staff had already started to make arrangements for a victory parade. First, he would visit Santo Tomas to meet with the ex-prisoners, and arrangements were made for his contingent to arrive at 9:00 in the morning of February 7. We all looked forward to seeing the great man and giving him our heartfelt thanks for our liberation.

Though just beginning, the occupation of Manila was going smoothly. Both the 1st Cavalry and the 37th Infantry had entered the outskirts of the city from the north, the Cavalry on February 3 on the northeast side, and the Infantry on February 5 on the northwest side, and accompanied by the element of surprise had met only light resistance. The 11th Airborne Division, diverted from its primary mission of capturing the southern end of Luzon, had advanced to the southern outskirts of Manila. However, the paratroopers met stiff resistance at Nichols Field, once an American Army airbase, and were being battered by small-arms fire and artillery that stopped their advance. As one Airborne company commander mockingly said, referring to the

Japanese naval troops who were defending the area, "Tell Halsey to stop looking for the Japanese Fleet, it's dying on Nichols Field."

The Japanese defenses were concentrated in a 5-mile swath from Nichols Field to a few hundred yards south and west of Santo Tomas on the north side of the Pasig River. They now prepared to consolidate their position and make a stand in the old walled city of the Intramuros and the adjacent business district with its large concrete buildings. Occupation of Manila was not going to be the easy mission that MacArthur anticipated. All hell was about to break loose.

EIGHTEEN

THE JAPANESE COUNTERATTACK

By the third day of liberation, Santo Tomas had become a full-fledged military encampment. A tank park emerged in the trees between the plaza and the Education Building, and an artillery battery emplacement sat in the field between the Education Building and Calle España. Troops were everywhere. They roamed the halls of the Main Building, often sitting in groups chatting with ex-prisoners. Of course, we all wanted to know what had been happening in the outside world and were eager to hear what the GIs could tell us.

For me, it was like living in Disneyland—all that military equipment just waiting to be inspected and soldiers happy to explain how everything worked. Seldom do civilians get to be so intimately involved with a military operation, such encampments usually being out of bounds. That day, I took full advantage of this unique access.

I started out by visiting the tank park and was invited to climb inside one of the armored vehicles. The driver showed me how the controls worked, the gunner showed me how he loaded his cannon and how he would fire it, and the tank commander let me sit in the turret hatch and showed me how his machine gun worked.

The next stop was to go into the Education Building, which was now in complete shambles after the firefight of the first evening of liberation. I gawked at the heavily damaged walls with barely any space that wasn't pitted by small arms fire. I went up to the third floor where the hostages had sheltered under their beds while the American rounds whizzed over their heads, and the Japanese guards joined them for protection. Both inside the building and outside along the road and field, small-arms cartridge casings littered the grounds. I gathered two pockets-full of 30 and 50-caliber brass. This was a wonderful addition to my shrapnel collection from the days of the bombings, and I was almost sick about the enormous quantity that I had to leave behind.

Then I walked through the field, plowed up by tank tracks, to the artillery battery. I stood and watched as the four guns executed a firing mission, holding my hands over my ears as they blasted shell after shell at some unseen enemy position. The artillerymen, shirtless, dirty, and sweating heavily under their metal helmets in the mid-day heat, worked rapidly and efficiently, loading the heavy shells into the breaches, and then standing away as one of them pulled the lanyard to fire the gun.

An artillery battery set up near the main Building of Santo Tomas executes a firing mission supporting American troops defending against Japanese positions in Manila. (Photo courtesy of Lou Gopal, producer of Victims of Circumstance.)

Standing behind the guns, I encountered a bonanza. Some of the bags of gunpowder had broken and were tossed aside, the pellets of propellant spilling out on the ground. I scooped up a couple of handfuls, and then wondered how I could carry them. My pockets were filled with brass casings, and I hit on the idea of pulling them out, then filling them with the gunpowder pellets before replacing them in my pockets.

I returned to our shanty, realizing I could always get more gunpowder at any time, and unloaded my hoard. I don't think my mother realized what all of those little pellets were, or she would have immediately confiscated and disposed of them. I just told her they were souvenirs, and she understood the collection of cartridge casings, but must have wondered why I would want to collect something that looked like a batch of rabbit droppings.

After lunch, I went with a friend to a place near the wall where there weren't any shanties nearby. We laid out a path of gunpowder and lit it. Matches were easy to get because the GI's got a pack of cigarettes and matches in their C-rations and were happy to give us a spare booklet. We were delighted with the way the flame raced along the gunpowder pathway, sparking and flashing as it went. Then we loaded a shell cartridge with gunpowder, laid a path of pellets to it, and lit that. It was even more satisfying as the flame lit into the cartridge, it took off like a rocket. This was going to provide endless entertainment!

Throughout the day, we heard explosions in the distance, and nearby, the occasional burst of machine gun fire or hammering of a Browning automatic rifle, interspersed with other small arms fire. We had become so accustomed to the constant sound of weapons firing that we no longer paid any attention. It was simply background noise like having a freeway running right behind your house, or having an airport landing path right above your roof. Eventually, the noise fades from your consciousness. When the noise becomes overwhelming, you briefly stop talking, then pick up again when it quiets, with little thought about what you are doing. We felt no threat from the activity going on outside our walls, because after all, we had the Army inside to protect us.

That evening after dark someone told me that I should go and look out of the windows on the west side of the Main Building. Since I was already on the third floor near my dormitory, I walked around the building in the peripheral hallways to one of the dormitories that looked west. The sight was amazing. The entire horizon seemed to be burning in an unbroken wall of flames. I later learned that the retreating Japanese had set fire to buildings and homes, creating a wall of fire to delay the advance of the American forces. Manila was not going to survive its second invasion of this war unscathed.

∞ ∞ ∞

The next day, February 7, we all looked forward with anticipation to General MacArthur's triumphal return to Manila. When I arose that morning, my mother made me put on a clean pair of shorts, shirt, and shoes. The shoes were pretty decrepit, with the front of the soles coming away from the shoes, but it was the best I could do. The three of us would go to the plaza together to see the general and hear what he had to say.

Before the great event, I went to the annex to get my breakfast and then returned to my dormitory. As I walked down the hallway towards the annex, I noticed a newly broken window and a hole gouged out of the concrete in the floor. It was almost in front of the dormitory next door to ours, and several people were lounging around the doorway. I casually asked them if they had found the shrapnel that had done the damage. They all shook their heads. No one had seen anything.

I then started to examine the broken concrete on the floor to see what I could find. In the midst of the debris was something that looked like concrete, but was smooth on one side. I reached down and picked it up, immediately dropping it as it burned my hand. What a wonderful large piece of shrapnel to add to my collection of much more modest pieces. It was about three inches across and weighed about one pound. I couldn't leave it there to cool, because the others had seen what happened and would immediately swoop down and grab it. The law of our little jungle was certainly a matter of possession equating to ownership, and I didn't yet have possession.

I stared down at this valuable treasure, my foot resting lightly on it, and a solution to my problem presented itself. I could slip the hot chunk of metal between the inner and outer soles of my shoe, and by shuffling along, get it to my dormitory where I could let it cool and take full possession. Here was a case where having disintegrating shoes turned out to be a boon.

I shuffled down to our dormitory, and my mother saw me coming, no doubt disgusted that I had already messed up my good clothes. But when I showed her my prize, which had cooled off enough to pick up, she was happy for me. I wonder to this day why she wasn't more curious about shrapnel coming into our hallway, and what the cause of it was. I can only conclude that we were so accustomed to the continual explosions and artillery fire, with stuff flying through the air, that we no longer gave thought to being an inadvertent victim. At least for me, it was part of the invincibility of the young.

Since MacArthur wasn't scheduled to arrive for another hour, I asked my mother if I could go outside and search for more shrapnel, and she agreed, as long as I was back in time to go to the ceremony with her and my sister. "And don't mess up your clothes!"

I skipped down the stairs and out into the plaza, then turned and headed towards the Gymnasium. When I got near the seminary, I noticed that the little chapel that was nearest the Main Building had been badly damaged. It looked like an artillery shell had hit the portico, and the front of the building was in shambles. I examined it with wonder because I hadn't heard a shell hit inside our campus, and no one else had mentioned it. Obviously, had we known, it would have been a hot topic of conversation. This apparently was where my hot chunk of shrapnel had originated.

I looked through the rubble and discovered several more large pieces of shrapnel lying there, far more than I could possibly carry. I picked up a piece as big as a saucer and several smaller pieces. These additions to my collection would make the ones collected during the bombing raids look puny indeed. I went back to our dormitory and showed my latest prizes to my mother. I explained where I'd been and she admired them, but never once did she question how come an artillery round had hit within the campus, nor did she express any concern that we were in any danger. Perhaps she was distracted by the thought that it was time to go to the plaza to see General MacArthur, or perhaps it was just our state of mind that we'd survive so much already that nothing worse could happen.

∞ ∞ ∞

The plaza was packed with people when we arrived. The general was driven into the campus in an Army staff car, which pulled to a stop at the entrance to the Main Building, almost in front of where we were standing. He got out of his car and made a few remarks to the crowd, while we stood right next to his car on the opposite side from where he stood. The area around and in front of us swarmed with reporters, photographers, and people shooting movie film.

My mother pushed me as close to the car as possible, and whispered that maybe my picture would be in one of the newspapers and my father would get to see me. The ceremony included draping an American flag, which one of the prisoners had kept hidden from the Japanese, off the portico to the main entrance. This moment was caught on film, and a big spread of the ceremony was featured in *Life Magazine*. However, when I later was able to examine those pictures, I never found my family or myself discernible in the mass of joyously celebrating people. Anyway, I doubt my father would have been able to recognize me since I'd changed so much in three and one-half years since he had last seen me.

A crowd of liberated prisoners congregates in the plaza in front of the Main Building to welcome General MacArthur. An hour later, after the crowd dispersed, the Japanese started shelling the camp. (Photo courtesy of Lou Gopal, producer of Victims of Circumstance.)

The ceremony was quite short, and MacArthur was driven away from the campus. Soon the plaza was almost completely deserted, except for a few military vehicles parked next to the Main Building and a scattering of people. I was still there with a friend, almost in the middle of the plaza, when there was a huge explosion. Debris and smoke flew from the west side of the building across the end of the plaza not far from where we were. Both of us fell to the ground, and when there was no second explosion, we got up and started to run for the entrance of the Main Building. I didn't realize until more than 60 years later that an Army Signal Corps photographer was taking background movie film, shooting across the plaza when the explosion occurred. He caught the debris flying from behind the building, and then zoomed in on my friend and me as we raced across the open space.

The first Japanese shell hits the Santo Tomas Main Building, the start of three days of bombardment that killed or wounded many liberated prisoners. (Photo courtesy of U.S. Army Signal Corps, 1945.)

Angus and a friend run for cover after the first shell hits the Main Building. (Photo courtesy of the U.S. Army Signal Corps, 1945.)

The Japanese had started to fight back. An incoming artillery round had exploded on the west side of the Main Building, the first of many shells aimed primarily at the Main and Education Buildings. The first round, unheralded, hit the chapel about 8:00 that morning. That one yielded many prized pieces of shrapnel for me. Then, for about two and one-half hours, the bombardment stopped. It remained quiet during the entire ceremony for MacArthur. Had the Japanese artillery observers been better, they could have inflicted immense damage to the crowd in the plaza, perhaps even killing the general. He had been a prime target since the war-opening bombing raid of December 8, 1941.

The shells came in at a slow rhythm, leaving time between each explosion. I soon learned to anticipate the interval between hits. I decided to join my mother and sister in our shanty. Timing the explosions, I waited in the rear lobby on the north side of the Main Building while the shells slammed into the west side. At a break in the shelling, I sprinted across the street and into the Annex. I exited at the far end and sprinted to the shanty. The shanty offered little or no protection from the shell fragments flying through the air. The three of us hastily beat a retreat back to the Annex and better shelter.

We remained sheltered in the central lobby of the Annex for the entire afternoon amid fellow ex-prisoners and several GIs. Most of the shells were hitting the Main Building on the wall adjacent to us. After each explosion, shell fragments and concrete pieces slammed against the corrugated iron of the siding and roof, rattling our senses. Had just one shell been off by fifty yards, it would have exploded squarely in our sanctuary.

Clearly there would be no lunch for us today, with the kitchen located in the most vulnerable place between the Main Building and the Annex. But the GIs shared some C-rations with us. Together, we waited and wondered how long the bombardment would go on, and the GIs assured us that our own artillery and aircraft would soon destroy the Japanese.

The interval between shell hits now stretched to about half an hour. A pretty girl who was with us, along with one of the

GIs, decided that it would be safe to go out to the patio for a smoke right after one of the shells hit. They had mistaken the timing because the next shell came much sooner than expected. The girl was hit in the face by a piece of shrapnel, and it sheared off her nose. Other GIs raced outside with a stretcher, and brought her back into our shelter, carrying her right past where I was sitting, the blood streaming down her face and all over her clothes. They took her into an aid station off the lobby to do what they could to stop the bleeding, and I didn't see her again until several weeks later. Her face had been horribly disfigured, but she had survived.

The shelling tapered off in the evening. After dark, we went back to our dormitory. Because of the exposure of the central kitchen, no meals were prepared, and we again ate the fare from the C-rations. I wasn't disappointed about that, because it was darned good solid food. I just didn't understand why the GI's complained when they had to eat it.

The next morning, the shelling took up once again, but it was now much less frequent. Our army had started to spot the Japanese artillery, and directed our own artillery and aircraft response. One of the Japanese artillery locations, on the roof of the Manila Hospital, was difficult to knock out without harming the staff and patients. The Japanese had no respect for civilian lives, and this was just another example.

A third day of shelling was even more intermittent, and by the end of the day, the last of the Japanese artillery had been knocked out. We could now all heave a sigh of relief, but it was time to count the damage. After surviving all of those years of imprisonment, 18 of our fellow prisoners had been killed, and 65 had been wounded. In addition, some of the soldiers and Filipino civilians who had been in the campus had also been killed.

After the shelling ended, I walked to the west side of the Main Building where most of the shells had struck. Enormous holes had been blasted through the concrete walls, and the dormitories were in chaos. The shower room where I usually went, which was on the northwest corner of the building near the Annex, had a hole blasted in it. The toilet stalls were all collapsed on each other, and blood still seeped across the tiles into the central drain, as someone must have been there when the shelling started. The dormitory on the first floor where we were housed when we first arrived in Santo Tomas had also been hit. If the accommodations had not been reorganized early on, when we moved to our dormitory near the southeast corner, we could easily have been killed.

It was chaos and confusion when the shelling first started. People in the dormitories on the side of the building that was targeted weren't even aware that they were in the direct path of the shells. As that day progressed, GI rescuers gathered nearby, and after a shell struck, they rushed into the dormitories and pulled the wounded out, with only a few minutes for their grisly work before the next incoming round arrived. They made their rescues so hastily that there was no time to bring out the dead, who they just stuffed into closets until they could come back later. After awhile, everyone was evacuated from that part of the building, and the killing diminished.

∞ ∞ ∞

In 1997, I returned to visit the University for the first time. It was a Sunday, and the Main Building was closed. My escorts, a bevy of young Filipinas who had graduated from the University of Santo Tomas, talked the head of security into letting us into the building. He personally escorted us as we explored through the halls that were still so familiar to me. I pointed to places where certain things had happened—where Lieutenant Abiko had lain dead, the dormitory where I had lived for more than three years, the hallway where a GI had shot himself while cleaning his side arm, and the dormitories that had been shattered by the shelling. I don't think any of the young people believed what I was telling them, so I suggested that we walk back to the plaza on the street that ran along the west side of the building. There, still clearly to be seen, were patches in the concrete, the newer material not yet weathered to match the material of the original building. It was from here that the scope of the devastation could best be viewed.

This last orgy of killing was particularly sad for some families. In one instance, the father had died of beriberi just weeks before the liberation, then the mother was killed in the shelling, leaving the two sons as orphans.

Camp life slowly returned to normal after the shelling ended, and the Army started to pull most of its units out of the campus. Some believed that the reason the Japanese shelled Santo Tomas was because it was a military encampment and a legitimate target. But the fact is that the shells were never aimed at the military targets such as the artillery battery and the tanks. Every one was aimed specifically at the civilian living quarters.

All across Manila the Japanese were fiercely resisting the American advance into the city. They fought block by block, and set anything that would burn on fire, creating walls of fire through which the GIs had to penetrate. Where large concrete buildings such as the Central Post Office existed, they turned them into multi-story pillboxes and fought for each floor as the Americans had to advance upward through the building to dislodge them. MacArthur's dream of a victory parade to celebrate his triumphal return died in the conflagration as the Japanese retreated across the Pasig River, blowing every bridge. In central Manila, they deeply entrenched themselves in the heavily walled Intramuros and the concrete buildings of the business district. This was just the start of the nastiest urban battle that the Americans had to fight in World War II.

NINETEEN

THE BATTLE OF MANILA

By the first week of February 1945, The Battle of Manila was in full sway. Most of the troops and tanks that had been on the campus returned to action. The artillery battery was moved to the northeast of us, judging from the number of artillery shells flying over our heads. The Japanese were entrenched across the Pasig River in the fortified old city, in the concrete buildings of the business district, and in the old High Commissioners residence. Most of their defenses were within an area of about a one-half mile arc drawn from the Manila Hotel, the closest point of which was not much more than a mile from us. The bay was on one side of their fortified enclave; on the other three sides, they faced the 37th Infantry, 1st Cavalry, and 11th Airborne Divisions. The Japanese were trapped as tightly as rats in a steel cage.

Now, the Japanese anger and frustration surfaced against the Filipinos, whose unswerving loyalty to America throughout the war had been so bitter to them. As they retreated, the Japanese burned whole blocks of buildings and homes. They went on an orgy of killing, shooting, and bayoneting people on the streets; entering hospitals to kill doctors, staff, and patients; and searching homes for victims. They cut off people's heads. They raped women and bayoneted babies. They shot people in the back. It was a repeat of the Rape of Nanking, for which they had been vilified by the League of Nations. Now it was the Manila Mur-

Filipinos in Manila suffered immensely during the battle and as result of the Japanese massacre. (Photo courtesy of Lou Gopal, producer of Victims of Circumstance.)

ders. In Fort Santiago, the headquarters for the Kempetai, prisoners were murdered on a wholesale basis. More than 600 people were herded into an underground cell and drowned when the tide came in. Of the 100,000 Filipinos killed during the Battle of Manila, it is estimated that the Japanese, in this orgy of killing, murdered 80,000. Others died because they were caught in the crossfire from the fierce fighting, trapped by the Japanese fortifications.

Japanese soldiers believed that surrender would bring great shame upon them and their families. Now that they were pariahs, they had no choice but to fight to the death. The old city, or Intramuros, surrounded by walls 10-feet high and 20-feet thick, was a warren of dug-in defensive positions, which ignored the safety of surviving civilians who were hiding in the thick-walled old buildings. The large concrete buildings in the business district, four to six stories high, were fortified with pillboxes and in-depth defenses. Positions were dug in around the High Commissioners residence in the hopes that the Americans would be reluctant to release an intensive bombardment on this icon of their colonial power.

With no way to cross, the two American divisions advancing from the north stalled when they reached the Pasig River. Heavy Japanese resistance also stalled the division advancing from the south. The Americans had no choice but to unleash an intense artillery barrage against these hardened positions. The Filipinos caught within the Japanese defenses could not escape this deadly fire, and it accounted for most of their casualties not directly attributable to murder.

∞ ∞ ∞

Our camp continued to house a fair number of GIs, but many were not billeted with us. Those who were provided essential services. Others were visitors taking a brief R&R from the battle and perhaps looking for relatives, friends, or friends of friends. All were armed and ready for any Japanese unit that might come out of hiding and attack.

We were close to the battlefront and could see the general area of fighting from the upper floors of the Main Building. American artillery unleashed a barrage—a constant sound of artillery and the sounds of explosions came so close together that I couldn't discern any gap in the sound. Day and night, I heard the crash of artillery firing and the whine of the shells passing overhead. The constant noise simply became background, and I continued my daily activities as if it wasn't there. It is hard for me to believe now that I could have been so unconcerned with what was going on around me. But to a young boy, it was an adventure and an education.

The camp kitchen had now converted over to serving K-rations, the rations the Army serves its troops when it can set up a field kitchen. I was really enjoying eating solid food again. I consumed such gourmet items as reconstituted powdered eggs, creamed chipped beef, often called SOS or shit on a shingle, Spam, bully beef served in a variety of ways, and all of the wonderful canned, packaged, and artificially prepared provisions Americans had developed as an expedient of war.

Years later when I was in college and living in a boarding house, my roommates would describe our food as something that would gag a maggot. Had they experienced the Army chow we were getting in Santo Tomas, they probably would have awarded it the same disdain, though, come to think of it, the food we got under the Japanese administration had killed more maggots than it gagged, and I'd eaten my fair share. But I loved Army chow, and even today, in a fit of nostalgia, I might cook a batch of SOS or corned beef with reconstituted dried mashed potatoes. I've heard from other ex-prisoners that they have the same reaction, some even opening a can of corned beef on the anniversary of Liberation Day just to lick the fat off the lid before devouring the rest of the contents.

∞ ∞ ∞

During the Battle of Manila, the field in the southwest corner in front of the Gym, where I had learned how to play baseball, became a cemetery for our fellow ex-prisoners killed in the Japanese shelling and for the GIs killed in the fighting. Day after day, more and more white markers were erected. The fighting was vicious and the casualties high.

On February 20, the force moving up from the south finally liberated the High Commissioners residence and now faced the heavily fortified concrete buildings in the business district. Forces attacking from the north had to make amphibious assaults across the Pasig River. On February 23, they finally crept through the nearly flattened walls of the Intramuros and in two days of building-to-building fighting dug out the last of the Japanese. Amid the carnage were many dead Filipinos, some showing signs of torture. Others locked in cells in Fort Santiago died of dehydration. When the troops finished that difficult mission, they turned their attention to digging the Japanese out of the business district.

The Americans were jungle fighters and had no experience in street fighting, but they learned and innovated as the battle progressed. The buildings in the business district presented a special challenge. First, GIs had to fight their way into the ground floor of each building. The Japanese then retreated to the next floor up, destroying the stairs and cutting holes in the floor to drop grenades on the Americans. GIs treated each floor as a new battleground until they got to the roof, and then they started over again on the next building.

It wasn't until March 3 that the last defenders succumbed. The Battle of Manila was one of the fiercest battles Americans fought during World War II, and it left the city a sea of rubble. Manila was one of the most destroyed cities of the war, second only to Warsaw. General Eichelberger, who commanded the southern force, exclaimed: "Man has ceased to exist except for some places that the Japanese thought were not worth defending or where American troops got in by surprise." We in Santo Tomas were very lucky that the flying column advanced so rapidly into the city. The Japanese had not yet had time to throw up their extensive defenses.

As I think back, those four weeks of battle seemed much longer, but it eventually ended. During the battle, our friends in the Los Baños camp also had been liberated in another dramatic surprise attack. This was the third of the "Great Raids" that started with the liberation of the Cabanatuan POWs on the day before the flying column launched its race to Manila.

On February 23, the 11th Airborne Division made a parachute drop right into Los Baños. At the same time, Filipino guerillas emerged from the jungle and attacked from outside the perimeter wire. The camp was quickly liberated without casualties, and the 2,200 prisoners were evacuated across the Laguna de Bay in armored amphibious tractors, under fire from counterattacking Japanese. Unfortunately, after the evacuation, the Japanese returned to Los Baños and slaughtered many of the Filipinos they believed helped the Americans, including burning a church where women and children had taken refuge. The extent of the Japanese's reprisals is still unbelievable to me. And yet today, I continue to see reports of Japanese legislators denying that they committed atrocities during the war.

∞ ∞ ∞

The Battle of Manila left the city as the second most destroyed city of World War II. (Photo courtesy of Lou Gopal, producer of Victims of Circumstance.)

Throughout the battle, I continued my routine around the campus. Although the fighting was within hearing distance, the relaxed attitude of the GIs in our camp helped to quell any apprehension I might have otherwise felt. We'd experienced our bit of action, and now the battle had moved on.

Someone once asked me whether I had been afraid during my years in Santo Tomas. I had to think about that really hard. I don't think I ever became actively afraid. That is one thing about being a kid, you don't perceive things the same way adults do. Even when I saw a victim of the Japanese shelling nearby and all covered in blood, my reaction was more, "Well isn't that interesting?" I think when you are constantly bombarded by noise and action, as we were for several weeks, your mind begins to perceive things differently.

However, all of that action obviously did penetrate my mind and have a lasting effect. After the fighting, I experienced a mild case of post-traumatic stress syndrome, though the term hadn't yet been invented in those days. I think back on how I reacted to certain things for a couple of years after the war and believe post-traumatic stress is the only explanation. It first appeared near the end of the Battle of Manila. The battle had moved about two miles away. Japanese artillery had been silenced, so they had only small arms to fight American tanks, artillery, and bombers. We were no longer threatened, but still within ear shot of the fighting.

It was a pleasant, balmy evening, as it can be so wonderfully so in Manila after the heat of the day has subsided. My mother, sister, and I were sitting in chairs outside of our shanty. We were joined by a couple of GIs. In the distance, we could hear a fighter-bomber make a diving attack on a Japanese position. There was that distinctive sound we were now so used to, as the engine roar increased in frequency when the bomber accelerated in its dive. I got very antsy and wanted to find a foxhole or bomb shelter to climb into. We heard the sound a second time. Again I was very nervous. One of the GIs noticed and said, "Don't worry. It's one of ours." I knew that, but logic didn't overcome that niggling anxiety.

Later, when I lived in England, I became very nervous whenever an airplane flew overhead, especially if it were at a low altitude. When I was at my school's playing field, I would want to duck into one of the nearby bomb shelters left over from the war. I remember a time when visiting my cousins in Southern England, we were exploring a cave cut into the bank of a stream. We were inside the cave when a plane flew over, and I remember feeling so comfortable being underground. It was like a return to the womb experience.

∞ ∞ ∞

After the battle, a calm descended on Santo Tomas, and we could count our losses. On Liberation Day, 3,768 prisoners were still on campus. During our confinement, the Japanese had executed seven prisoners. More than 450 had died of natural causes, such as starvation and disease. After liberation, 19 died as a result of enemy action, bringing our total losses to approximately 476 people.

Although I was nine and one-half years old, I think I aged a few years through the experiences of the last few months. I also think that this was true of most of the children, who now had a very different way of viewing life. I believe I was less exuberant and more introspective. But many of us who had gone through the same experience came away with positive effects. I noticed after seeing fellow internees again years later, they too seemed to have a very upbeat outlook on life.

∞ ∞ ∞

When it was safe to do so, my mother, sister, and I walked out of the main gate of Santo Tomas. For me it was the first time in two and one-half years that I'd been outside the walls. This part of the city did not show a lot of damage, because the flying column occupied it before the Japanese prepared defenses. We saw the results of a few artillery shells and a fair amount of small arms pitting, but no wholesale damage. As we walked down Calle España, the Filipinos who were setting up shops or on the streets smiled and waved to us.

Our walk took us westward, and after a short distance, Calle España intersected with another main street. Just off this street was the old Bilibid prison. We walked through the arched concrete gate into a courtyard. Large doors opened into the gray-stone prison building. We stepped through the doors into an anti-room beyond which was the dark interior of the prison with its iron-barred cages. I could easily see that our confinement in Santo Tomas, though crowded, was nothing like the stark horror the military prisoners suffered.

It was easy to see why the American administration, before the war, had replaced Bilibid with the new penitentiary at Mult-inlupa. However, when I returned to Manila for the 60th anniversary of the liberation, I wanted to return to Bilibid to see if it still looked as terrifying as it did at the end of the Japanese era.

To my surprise, I discovered that visits were not possible because the Filipinos were again using the prison. If ever there was an incentive to be an honest person in the Philippines that would be it.

∞ ∞ ∞

Now, more interesting things were beginning to happen. Most of us were thinking of going home. I'm not sure what going home really meant to me. I knew we couldn't go back to Tientsin. My mother said we would go to her parent's home in England and wait for the war to end, after which we could start to rebuild our broken lives.

Every week, a list of names would be read on the public address system of those people to be included on the next repatriation ship. One day I heard our names read and knew that we soon would leave for America. What a thrill for me, to look forward to the long sea voyage, seeing America for the first time, then the trip back to England. I didn't know what to expect of England. I only remembered the last time we were there on vacation and the European war had only just begun. But my mother considered it her home, even though she hadn't lived there for almost 15 years. Her excitement was infectious, so I was excited too.

We didn't have the proper clothes for a long sea voyage or for the cooler climate my mother said we could expect in America. She could probably imagine me arriving on the Golden Shores dressed in a ragged pair of shorts, threadbare shirt, and shoes with the soles coming off. It was not a picture she wished to contemplate, though it wouldn't have meant a hoot to me. The American Red Cross came to our rescue with a shipment of clothes. The clothes were available in the plaza. When we went there to outfit ourselves, we found several tables pushed together with a hodge podge of clothes dumped on them. Although we were free to take what we wanted, I'm sure the Red Cross would have loved to charge us if we'd had any money.

The Red Cross had apparently emptied the ragbags of America to bring us these sartorial treats, most of which dated back to the depression era. We pawed through the stacks of well-worn clothing to find something that fit. I eventually found a pair of trousers and a long-sleeve shirt that were close to my size, if a little big. At another table, I found a pair of high-top Keds sneakers. My prize, though, was an overseas cap that I believe dated to World War I. But it was military, and it made me very proud to wear. When we were all outfitted, we could have starred in a poster appeal of Appalachians for the Tennessee Valley Project. Now we were ready to leave this place, and after almost three and one-half years of imprisonment, what possible new adventures could remain?

TWENTY

LEAVING SANTO TOMAS

Once we received notice to be on the next repatriation ship, the days seemed to drag forever as we awaited the great day. Many people already had left the camp, and I felt we were among the last to leave because the Americans had priority. I discovered later that wasn't true. In fact, many Americans left after us, and the last of the people to be repatriated didn't leave until August. Though it seemed like one of the longest periods we had to endure in Santo Tomas, it actually was only four weeks from the end of the Battle of Manila until we were shipboard. Still another adventure awaited me.

We finally sailed on April 2, the day after my mothers 41st birthday. What a wonderful birthday present. We assembled in the plaza early in the morning and were given a cardboard tag on which to write our name, the name of our ship, and our shipboard accommodations. We tied the tag to a buttonhole, so it could be easily read as we boarded. I was a bit miffed by this because it made me feel like I was simply a package being mailed, but I followed instructions. I didn't want to be left behind.

We boarded a bus in the plaza, carrying our suitcases, which had served as our cupboard drawers under our bunks for the last three years. Along with my most precious possessions, I packed my long pants and shirt and some underwear. I wore shorts and a short-sleeve shirt with my high-top tennis shoes. Into a 90-millimeter brass shell casing, I put my now large collection of shrapnel and small-arms cartridge cases. That made the suitcase pretty heavy, but I was darned if I was going to leave behind the only souvenirs I collected during my extended stay in Manila.

As we drove down the long driveway to the main gate, I looked back to see Santo Tomas for the last time, until I returned on a visit more than 50 years later. On each of the two occasions that I did return, I was amazed how little the campus had changed, while at the same time how much of what had once been open space was filled by new buildings and crowded with students. In 1997, when next I saw Santo Tomas, the Annex and Infirmary were gone, replaced with large buildings. Now, the battered Education Building was a research hospital. Where our shanty had stood was a theater in a complex of new buildings. The little chapel next to the Seminary—the first unfortunate target of the Japanese shelling—was now a large church. But, the patched-up Main Building looked so much the same that it was as if I'd just driven around the block in that bus and had returned the same day, though my dormitory was now a research laboratory and the cots were replaced with laboratory benches.

The bus turned right from the main gate onto Calle España. We traveled past the Bilibid prison and then turned left towards the Pasig River. From this vantage point, we could see the fruits of the Battle of Manila. Fierce fighting had taken place at the old Central Post Office just beyond Bilibid, and there were many damaged buildings along our route. When we reached the river, I noticed that the bridge was a wreck of twisted steel, its span broken and resting in the river.

We turned right and drove parallel to the river, passing other wrecked bridges on one side and destroyed buildings on the other side. Ahead, on the far side of the river, we saw Fort Santiago, the anchor of the Intramuros near the mouth of the Pasig River. Its once massive walls were reduced to rubble. Nowhere was one block of stone still standing upon another. A sea of devastation lay inside the walls. The once beautiful old city surrounded by its massive wall was reduced to a random sea of stone and brick, with no complete building standing and only the shell of what had once been a cathedral showing above the devastation.

The bus continued along the river, then turned left and slowly crossed it on a pontoon bridge built by the Army. We were on a street that ran between the harbor and the Intramuros, and we now had a closer view of the total devastation. The over 400-hundred-year-old walled city no longer existed, except as a pile of rubble. Further ahead, we could see the newer business center. All that was left were gutted and burned concrete shells of buildings. For all intents and purposes, the city once called the "Pearl of the Orient" no longer existed.

It seemed impossible that the city could ever recover from such a catastrophe. Indeed, the Intramuros remained a wasteland until 1978. Then the indomitable spirit of the Filipino people rose above the disaster, and the Philippine government started its restoration. When I returned in the mid-1990s, any sign of the total destruction was rare. The walls had been rebuilt, the buildings restored, and a community of people lived in it and celebrated the Intramuros rebirth. Even Fort Santiago on the river side of the community had been lovingly restored; and aside from a brass plaque, no one would know that it had once been the headquarters of the feared and hated Japanese Kempetai and a place of torture and death for thousands of Filipino and Allied prisoners. The city center was also thriving, packed with people on the sidewalks, stores, and businesses, with constant traffic jams from the hordes of vehicles that populated its streets. It was another world from what I saw when I left Manila so many years ago.

∞ ∞ ∞

Our bus turned away from the destruction and drove onto a pier. Tied alongside was a large gray ship that was to be our transport to America. We stood on the pier with our suitcases in a crowd of other people. A number of people in uniform checked tags and sorted people into groups. While I waited, I took the opportunity to inspect the ship, which I wouldn't again be able to see from this perspective until we disembarked in America.

From the pier, the ship appeared enormous. It is an illusion that I learned later to discount, because as large as a ship seems when docked, it becomes small and insignificant when it is cast out on the infinite ocean. The *S.S. John Lykes*, owned and operated by the Lykes Shipping Company, was under lease to the U.S. Army as a troop transport. Above the bow was a gun tub with two three-inch guns. Next came two hatches to the forward holds, with a mast and booms between them. Then the island rose up above the deck and was topped by a squat funnel. Several 20-millimeter guns were mounted along the decks on the island. Behind the island was another hatch, for the after hold, along with another mast and booms. And on the very stern was another gun tub with a 4-inch gun.

By today's standards, the ship was relatively small: 418-feet long and 5,028 gross tons, and configured to carry 1,288 troops. It was a Maritime Commission design similar to the Liberty and Victory ships being turned out by American shipyards at an incredible rate, except this design had a higher top speed.

One of the first ships to repatriate liberated prisoners directly to America was the John Lykes with Angus and his family on board. (Photo courtesy of the United States Maritime Commission.)

As I stood gawking at this monster, someone came by and checked my baggage tag, then directed me to join a small group standing near the gangplank. My mother and sister joined a different group. Shortly, a uniformed sailor led us up the gangplank onto the main deck. We walked forward on the steel deck, then through a doorway and down a steep stairway into the number two hold, which was just forward of the island.

We were told to pick a bunk and put our suitcase on it, then we were free to go topside and explore. The canvas bunks were stretched across steel pipe stanchions and stacked five high. Each bunk held a blanket, kapok pillow, and a kapok life vest. Only a few people from Santo Tomas were in this hold, so almost all of the bunks were available. With my love for sleeping as high as possible, I picked the top rack in the stack.

I went topside and thoroughly explored the entire length of the main deck, discovering my mother and sister near the port bow. Having learned from the overcrowded conditions in Santo Tomas, my mother had claimed a patch of deck next to the railing by laying out a blanket and putting her personal belongings on it. This was to become our home base for the entire voyage, and, particularly in the tropics, a sanctuary from the oppressive heat in the holds.

The men and boys bunked in holds one and two in front of the ship's island. My mother, sister, and all of the other women had been assigned to hold three aft of the island. The island itself was off limits to us. The ship's and military officers took those accommodations. However, the main deck level of the island housed the mess hall, a place of great delights, as we were soon to start eating ship's rations.

Peering over the side, I noticed that trucks were arriving and unloading soldiers. They started up the gangway carrying their duffle bags, and I soon learned that our hold was not going to be almost empty, but would have a large contingent of soldiers. For me to meet these new passengers was an absorbing experience because they were battle-hardened veterans of the jungle fighting in New Guinea, the Solomon Islands, and the Philippines finally heading home after long tours of duty. At first they were quiet and not very communicative, but as the voyage lengthened and we neared home, they became ever more exuberant.

Finally, all passengers were aboard, and the last cargo was hoisted and stored. By late afternoon, we were ready to sail. On board were about 500 ex-prisoners from Santo Tomas and an equivalent number of GIs, not a full load, but plenty to keep the deck space crowded. However, the ship was designed to carry more, so our accommodations in the hold were only partly filled. There was no problem with the toilet facilities, and the lines for chow were reasonable. Many people who have traveled on a troop ship think they are terribly uncomfortable and boring, but this was a luxury cruise compared to what we had just left.

∞ ∞ ∞

Late in the afternoon, the *John Lykes* eased away from the dock and slowly threaded its way into Manila Bay. Eagerly, I leaned over the rail to watch every detail of the departure. In the vicinity of the docks, the bay was filled with the detritus of war. Ship after ship lay sunk beneath these waters, only part of their hulls, their superstructures, or their masts showing. Our ship twisted and turned along a narrow passage blasted between these hulks. It seemed to me that I could have walked from one side of the bay to the other without ever getting my feet wet.

The next time I sailed into Manila Bay, the surface of the water was free of any indication of the terrible toll on shipping Japanese bombers took in 1941 and the Americans in 1944 and 1945. On that occasion, another passenger was on deck with me in the early morning, and I told him what we were seeing—on this side Bataan, over there Cavite, and ahead the main harbor with the Intramuros as a backdrop. We used his navigation chart to orient the various landmarks. On it were marked the symbols of shipwrecks, all that was left of that mass of twisted steel I saw when I last departed the tortured city.

That evening we passed Corregidor as we exited Manila Bay and joined a convoy being assembled for the voyage to the

United States. Fifty years would pass before I would see this scene again. This time I'd be sailing on a great white cruise ship in the lap of luxury, instead of a crowded gray troop ship. But what was ahead in 1945, I would soon find, was a whole different world from what I was leaving.

TWENTY ONE

WELCOME TO AMERICA

As the *John Lykes* sailed slowly out of Manila Bay, chow call came over the intercom, and I headed to the mess hall. I carried my newly issued aluminum mess kit and canteen cup; and on that first evening, I put it to good use. A GI showed me how to take the lid off and fit it on the handle. It essentially became a small tray with two compartments in the lid and one large compartment in the base, all with a lip about one and one-half inches deep. I can see now that this must have been the inspiration for the TV dinner. The GI told me to stick the knife, fork, and spoon in my shirt pocket. Now I was ready to brave the hazards of the food line.

Following my advisor, I walked down the line while the row of GIs who were on KP took aim and with amazing accuracy hit my new friend's plate with a slab of meatloaf, then a scoop of mashed potatoes, followed by gravy, and then peas. Into the lid went a roll and a square of sheet cake. Finally, a GI wielding a fork with one bent tine speared a pat of butter, and with a spoon behind it, launched the butter at the mess kit with a snap of his wrist. It was poetry in motion, the whole serving process taking no more than five seconds, the food hitting his mess kit with accuracy, almost every part of the meal going into the proper compartment. In the course of a meal, 1,000 people were served in this way.

Being shorter than my new friend, I was a more challenging target; and since I wasn't going to be assigned to KP duty, there was no fear of retaliation. When I got to the narrow tables with bench seats bolted to the deck, gravy decorated my shirt, cake and peas rested in a sodden mass, my roll was submerged in the mashed potatoes, and meatloaf was somehow resting on top of my butter. But I wasn't complaining. It was real food and tasted heavenly. By the time I fished my cake out of the remaining peas, I was more than stuffed.

Now I was faced by a moral dilemma. I had eaten less than half of what had been tossed in my mess kit, so what could I do with the leftovers? There was enough food left that, if I'd added a few cups of water, would have been the equivalent of several days of meals during my imprisonment. My GI friend had eaten almost everything on his mess kit, and now looked over and saw my dilemma. "Come on," he said, "I'll show you what we do."

I followed him to an almost overflowing garbage can and watched as he scraped his mess kit into it. I stood looking down into that can filled with perfectly good food, and ached to know how much good food was wasted while we had been starving. Finally, with a little encouragement from the GI, I cleaned out my kit. Then I followed him to where three garbage cans sat, each filled with steaming water. I dunked my kit and implements in the first one, which cleared the remains of the food, then I dipped it in one filled with steaming soapy water, and finally rinsed it in the last one. Easy, the dishes were done and I closed the mess kit and cup, ready for my next meal.

I went on deck to our territory and sat with my mother and sister. The night was balmy with a light breeze and a million stars hanging over our heads as our ship moved slowly, maintaining its position in the forming convoy. Looking over the side, I could see a slight luminescence in the water from our bow wave. Soon my eyes felt heavy, and I started to fall asleep. I decided to go to my bunk in the hold and headed down the staircase, which I had been told was really called a ladder.

As I lay on the stretched canvas of my bunk, my head on the kapok pillow, I was sweating and uncomfortable. I wasn't going to be able to sleep under these conditions, so I went back up the ladder and to our blanket spread on the deck. I laid down and soon fell fast asleep.

When I awoke in the morning, the convoy had formed up and was under way in the open ocean. Our ship was gently rolling and pitching in an unfamiliar motion. My stomach started to feel queasy, so I crawled over to the gunnels and stuck my head over the side to look at the bow wave. Shortly, my rebelling stomach gave up its contents, and I donated what was left of last night's dinner to the fish. A few minutes later, I felt fine again and was ready for the challenges of the breakfast line. That early morning was the only time I was sea sick on the entire 31-day voyage.

∞ ∞ ∞

Our convoy of about 50 ships sailed neatly aligned in parallel columns. A screen of destroyer escorts patrolled around the edges like hungry wolves. Our speed was abysmally slow. The entire convoy could travel only as fast as the slowest ship, which was probably no more than six knots. Strangely, we were sailing south, rather than northeast, where America lay.

Even though the Japanese fleet had been largely destroyed in the Battle of Leyte Gulf, many surface warships survived and submarines still harried Allied shipping in the western Pacific. Our course took us through the Philippine Islands, across the equator, and to our first landfall at New Guinea. The *John Lykes* docked for a day at New Hollandia to take on more supplies to feed the large number of hungry passengers; the larder had to be restocked. The next leg, still achingly slow, took us north to Hawaii, where we finally dropped the convoy and sped along on our own to the west coast of America.

∞ ∞ ∞

On our first morning at sea, the captain ordered an abandon-ship drill. We were to report to our assigned emergency stations wearing our kapok life jackets and remain there until ordered to abandon ship. If that order came, we were to jump overboard. Life rafts stowed in various places on the ship would be released into the water. We then should swim to a raft and board it. In the explanation, it all seemed so straightforward and easy that there was no reason to worry. Nothing was said about floating or burning oil, the difficulties we might encounter if the ship were still under attack, or how stormy weather would affect the procedure.

Following the drill, we watched a movie in the mess hall that illustrated the abandon-ship procedure. It included a segment on what to do if sharks attacked, explaining that you could scare the sharks away by splashing vigorously and releasing shark repellent. Of course, no shark repellent was available, so there was all the more incentive to splash vigorously. Research on shark behavior since that time has proven that splashing was exactly the wrong thing to do because this action mimics a wounded animal and is an attraction for sharks to attack. I often wonder how much this bad advice contributed to the many deaths of seamen on the cruiser *Indianapolis* when it was torpedoed on its way to the Philippines after delivering the first atomic bomb to Tinian a few weeks after we completed our voyage across the Pacific.

After these special events, we fell into a routine for the entire voyage. Aside from our three square meals a day, the most important daily event occurred at noon when a news report was read over the ship's public address system. In Europe, Germany's defenses were collapsing under the Allied advance from the south and the west and the massive assault by the Russians from the east.

The GIs cheered when it was announced that the Americans and Russians had met at the Elbe River. I cheered along with them, though I really didn't understand the significance of that cautious contact that ended the Allied eastward thrust in that sector and became the demarcation line that later so bitterly divided Europe. We still considered the Russians our friends and allies at that time, but it was only a few months later, after the final defeat of Germany, that British Prime Minister Winston Churchill commented, "I think we've killed the wrong pig."

On board ship, I had lots of opportunity for games and play. The deck was covered with little houses, vents, and appurtenances to be explored and to be used in games of hide and seek and various other activities. At night, when submarines couldn't follow floating debris to track the convoy, crewmen collected the trash and threw it overboard. Sorting through it, I found all kinds of treasures. One favorite activity was to take wood from the food crates and carve propellers that would rotate wildly in the wind. Overall, I had plenty to do to keep me occupied, and the time went quickly.

In the tropics, days can be unbearably hot and nights warm and sticky. Occasional rain showers were welcome in the daytime, although a nuisance at night when I slept on deck. Fresh water was limited, so the water from taps and showers provided salt water only. It was difficult to get lather in the shower, but that didn't really worry me; I wasn't too inclined to scrub with soap anyway. But I did spend a lot of time in the shower because there was unlimited hot water. Someone had brought a 55-gallon oil drum into the shower room. We filled it with water and had a great time jumping in for a full immersion with lots of splashing around. Though this was kids play, the GIs didn't seem to mind and often horsed around with us.

When we approached the equator, several passengers wanted to hold the traditional ceremony of Neptune's Court, where all people who have never crossed the equator before are brought before the court and hazed and then dunked in a large tub of water. The party never got off the ground, though, because the captain believed there were far too many people on board. Instead, we received a certificate attesting to the fact that we'd met King Neptune's requirements and were now qualified members of the court. We received a similar certificate later when we crossed the International Date Line.

We docked for one day at New Hollandia, but no one was allowed off the ship. Some natives wandered by between the dock and the jungle. They were most strange looking. Wearing only a loincloth of woven grass, they were completely black and had huge fuzzy heads of hair. The GIs derisively called them "fuzzy wuzzies." In the 1960s, some children of these GIs adopted the hairstyle as a form of rebellion against their parents and society, except it came to be called an Afro.

It was extremely hot, and huge deluges of rain punctuated the day. At first I went to the hold for shelter, but it was unbearably hot and humid, so I spent the rest of the day on deck and just got soaked. It seemed like everyone adopted the same philosophy. Finally we were at sea again, and our convoy headed north through the trackless Pacific Ocean.

This was "Indian Country," and the destroyer escorts tightened up the formation. All ships set up for a live-fire practice. As the time approached, the Navy gun crews, rigged out in life jackets and helmets, manned their guns. At the appointed time, one of the 3-inch guns fired and was immediately echoed by the chatter of 20-millimeter guns. Then another of the big guns fired and again was followed by the chatter of the lighter guns. This syncopation continued for about half an hour. The sound reverberating off the steel plates of the ship was deafening, far worse than the firing and explosions of artillery during the battle of Manila.

Not only were the guns on our ship firing, but also the guns on every other ship in the convoy. I couldn't tell where the shells from all of these ships were falling, and being in an outer column of the convoy, I surely hoped they were all going over us. If the convoy was ever attacked, I wondered where all of that steel going up in the air would eventually fall. We'd probably do more damage to our own ships than the Japanese would.

∞ ∞ ∞

A few days after leaving New Hollandia, April 14 by our calendar, we all gathered on our favorite perches for the noon news. I was on the top of a house containing the derrick operating machinery between the two forward hatches, which was a favorite location for many GIs. Expecting to hear more good news about the advance on Berlin, the first bulletin was a complete shock: President Roosevelt had died the previous day in Warm Springs, Georgia. The newsreader paused, and there was total silence except for the wind through the rigging. Then someone sobbed. All around me stood tough GIs with tears streaming down their faces. The people loved this jaunty president who had led the country out of the Great Depression, directed the military buildup, and commanded the armed forces that diligently smashed the German and Japanese war machinery.

A few days later, another tragedy struck. A small child of a couple from Santo Tomas died. Weakened by the poor nutrition in the camp, the child had not fully recovered, and medical facilities were not available on the *John Lykes* to overcome the child's failing system. With no place to keep the remains, the child was given a burial at sea according to maritime tradition. A ceremony was held on the after hatch, and the captain read the service. Then the small bundle was tipped over the rail at the stern and dropped into the waves to disappear forever. When we arrived off Honolulu on April 24, the ship stopped briefly. A small boat came alongside and the parents of the child disembarked to go ashore.

∞ ∞ ∞

In Hawaii, our convoy broke up, and we were on our own for the last leg of the journey to the West Coast. Our destination had changed. We now would land in Los Angeles instead of San Francisco. The *John Lykes* steamed away from the lush tropical islands. No longer impeded by the convoy, it could show its class, speeding up to twelve knots. In just seven days we would be in America.

The GIs, who had been quiet and introspective as we left Manila, now opened up at the prospect of soon being home. They started talking about what they would do when they returned to their hometowns, especially what they were going to eat after suffering for so long eating Army chow. I listened carefully and concluded that the preference was for a thick juicy hamburger, whatever that was. I had never seen or tasted a hamburger, but from the loving descriptions I heard, I just knew it had to be something delicious, maybe even better than a plate of beans. I was now getting plenty of beans in the ship's mess hall.

As we headed north, the days became cooler, and no longer was it comfortable to sleep out on the deck. The temperature in the hold was now quite pleasant. In fact, I was happy to climb to my top bunk to spend the night.

While sleeping soundly one night, the raucous sound of the alarm klaxon warning everyone to go to their abandon ship stations jolted me awake.

The GIs in the bunks around me groaned and complained that it was just a nuisance to have a drill in the middle of the night. They wanted to skip the drill and go back to sleep. Well, if the GIs weren't concerned, there was no need for me to be, so I rolled over and tried to go back to sleep. The sounds of running feet and shouts coming from above kept me awake. The slamming and toggling of watertight doors soon followed. Finally I got to sleep in the eerie quiet.

Unconcerned that I'd skipped the drill, I sauntered up to deck in the morning and went to our space by the rail. My mother was furious. Why had I not come on deck when the alarm sounded? I explained that the GIs in my hold had just not thought it was worth the trouble to attend the drill.

Then, with great intensity, she told me that it was not a drill! During the night, the ship's watch had seen a submarine on the surface. When they flashed the recognition signal on the communication lamp, the submarine had not responded. The crews for the 3- and 4-inch guns tracked the submarine, waiting either for the proper coded reply or for the order to fire and sink it. The submarine was on a course that was the reverse of ours and we were approaching bow-on. The submarine kept coming closer, and still no signal. Then it quietly slipped past our port side not a hundred yards away and slowly faded into the dark astern of us.

I could just imagine the radio operators on our ship trying desperately to get an explanation from the headquarters of NAV-SUBPAC of whether they had a submarine heading to Hawaii from the West Coast, and the Naval authorities being reluctant to say anything definitive to the Merchant Marine. If the submarine was American, I could imagine the skipper scrambling around trying to locate the code book to respond to the recognition signal, using very creative language to berate his yeoman. Or if the submarine was Japanese, he was no doubt saying a prayer to his ancestors that the *John Lykes* would not fire on him. It sounds like just another SNAFU (situation normal, all fouled up), bad judgments that during the war caused many innocent engagements and deaths.

The submarine sighting was never explained, and we'll never know whether it was friend or foe. But as my mother explained to me, I was locked below deck, and if the submarine had fired a torpedo, I'd have gone down with the ship.

∞ ∞ ∞

In the predawn hours of May 2, everyone aboard ship who could assembled on deck. In the dim light, we could see the low hills of the mainland. America at last!

It was full light when we approached Angel's Gate, the entrance through the breakwater into the Los Angeles harbor. The air was chilly and a gray overcast pressed down on us. To the north, a barren brown hill rose into the cloud; to the east lay the narrow entrance to San Pedro Channel. The ship slowed to what seemed like a frustratingly imperceptible speed. After 31 days on the *John Lykes*, we were all impatient to get past the last three or four miles to our dock.

We entered the narrow channel, barely moving, the busy docks and concentration of ships along both sides slowly drifting astern. The bustling little town of San Pedro rose abeam on the port side, seeming to climb up a series of low bluffs to the base of the hill. It was a rough town and a seaman's paradise, full of bars and brothels. Slowly, we put the center of town behind us and turned into the West Basin. It seemed like another forever as the ship moved alongside the pier and moored.

As we moored, a band on the dock played patriotic favorites, and a crowd of people stood nearby waved and shouted. The GIs screamed back when they saw someone they recognized. It was very stirring and emotional, but no one was waiting on the dock for us.

With the gangway secured, the GIs streamed ashore for reunions with their families, as did a few of the people from Santo Tomas. Those seeing their loved ones for the first time in years felt great joy. Then the families slowly drifted off. Most of the GIs boarded trucks and were driven away. All that remained on the *John Lykes* were the rest of the people from Santo Tomas, wondering how the world had changed in all those years we had been gone.

I now live on that brown hill, the first sign of mainland America we had seen from the ocean. It has changed, covered with homes and green from cultivated gardens and trees. From our home near the top, I can look down on the Los Angeles harbor, trace the channel that had seemed impossibly long, and see the very dock where I first stepped ashore in America. Much has happened in the ensuing years, but nothing in America has ever surpassed the excitement of that gray day so long ago.

TWENTY TWO

ONWARD TO ENGLAND

Finally, it was our turn to go ashore from the *John Lykes*, and I eagerly skipped down the gangway to step on American soil for the first time. We boarded buses that took us to a reception center in Los Angeles where we could meet friends and relatives or make travel arrangements.

The ride took about an hour across an endless flat plain, heavily cultivated with beans, strawberries, and other low-growing crops. After awhile, the fields became interspersed with small white-painted clapboard homes. Through the gray haze, we could see the buildings of the central city. They were not tall buildings, but they were densely packed. When we entered the downtown area, we saw many pedestrians, a few cars, and red trolleys that ran on tracks in the streets.

We stopped in front of a building with an ornate façade and an "Elks Club" sign displayed on the side. A reception committee directed us to a large room where a crowd of people watched as we came through the door. I felt like the proverbial deer in the headlights, or perhaps an elk. The crowd, friends and relatives of the people from Santo Tomas, rushed to greet us and showered us with hugs, kisses, and tears.

A tall soldier walked over to us and said, "Elsie? Elsie is that you?" And then he rushed to my mother and hugged her, finally turning to hug my sister, then me. It was John, the brother I hadn't seen in four years, since he left for Shanghai to go to college during that last summer in Tientsin. How much we had changed, especially my mother, that he had to ask that first tentative question when he first saw us. He too had changed, seeming taller, more mature, and very handsome in his Army uniform.

Now came a rush of talk as we tried to catch up with our lives. Several days passed before we exhausted our stories and heard about John's adventures with the Chinese guerillas and the Flying Tigers. John was now stationed in Washington, D.C., and the home office of American International Underwriters had arranged for him to meet us. They also arranged for us to go to New York and from there to England until the war was over and we could rejoin my father.

Right now, though, the first order of business was lunch. John had a car and driver waiting outside. As we got into the sedan, he asked the driver to take us to a convenient restaurant, and he drove to a nearby drive-in, at that time the ultimate in fine dining in Los Angeles.

My mother, sister, and I stared at the list of choices on the menu. For the first time since we entered Santo Tomas, we actually were going to choose what we wanted to eat. The whole process was confusing and somewhat overwhelming. How could I choose whether I wanted a steak fried by a chicken, or something the French dipped, or a melted patty? What were these things? Then I saw "hamburger." At that, my choice was made for me. I remembered how the GIs described this delicacy in loving detail. To be honest, when it was served, I wasn't sure where the romance was in this huge thing that was mostly bun, but I loved the greasy French fries cooked in pure lard. After lunch, the driver dropped us off at our hotel, where John was also staying.

We still had a couple of days to spend in Los Angeles before taking a train to New York. During that time, the people from the local office of AIU made us welcome, invited us to dinner, and showed us around LA and Hollywood.

∞ ∞ ∞

On the morning of May 4, we boarded a transcontinental train. We had two first-class Pullman compartments, one for my mother and sister, while John and I shared the other. At the time, I didn't question how we rated such special treatment in the middle of the war, when it was very difficult for ordinary people to get train reservations. It wasn't until many years later that I found out the head of AIU, and my father's boss before the war, was also the head of the Office of Strategic Services (OSS) operations in Asia. That bit of information clarified where the influence originated for our VIP status.

When we arrived in Chicago on May 7, we had to change trains for the last leg of our trip to New York City. Since we had a few hours to spend, we left the station to explore Chicago.

Early that morning in France, the Germans signed an unconditional surrender, and the war in Europe was finally over. Celebrating throngs packed the streets. Much to John's embarrassment, every girl we passed grabbed and kissed him, his uniform acting like a magnet. We were happy too, but the defeat of Germany was only the first step in the difficult task that lay ahead. To defeat Japan would be an enormous challenge.

The next morning, we pulled in to Grand Central Station in New York. Again, AIU had arranged a hotel for us in Manhattan, and the people in the head office treated us to luncheons and dinners and parties in their homes high up in those towering skyscrapers.

On several occasions, I heard them complaining about rationing and other restrictions as a result of the war. Yet when they invited us to dinner, they served huge portions with large slabs of meat and rich desserts that I couldn't finish. At cocktail parties, there seemed no limit to the booze and fancy canapés being served. And they could enjoy any restaurant, without restriction, to dine on prime rib, lobster, Chinese food, or hamburgers. Somehow their complaints didn't ring true, and I wonder if they were just raising these issues to convince us that they too had suffered from the war.

We were quite overwhelmed. Neil Starr, head of AIU, offered us the use of his estate near Brewster in upstate New York. John couldn't join us; he had to report back for duty in Washington. When he left to take the train south, we had an emotional parting. We understood the war was still on and he had duties to perform, but we had no idea when we would see him again.

Shortly after he left, a chauffeur picked us up in a large black Cadillac limousine and drove us to the country. We left Manhattan and the concrete jungle that was the city and traveled north on a parkway along the Hudson River, then through some beautiful country with rolling hills and lakes, resplendent in its bright green spring foliage. Traffic was light, but as our chauffeur explained, gasoline rationing limited traffic, and many people in the city used public transportation and didn't need a car.

The Starr estate was enormous, with several servants to take care of the house and grounds. They were quite solicitous and made our stay very enjoyable. I explored the immense grounds, went swimming when they filled the swimming pool, visited the village so that we could shop and see the sights, and went sailing on a nearby lake. These were the most pleasant days I spent in America. The icing on the cake was the morning that an RAF officer we had met in the City flew over at a very low level in a Spitfire. He waggled the wings and waved at me as I stood in the driveway. He reminded me so much of that last day as a prisoner in Santo Tomas when the SBD had flown over and dropped the message of hope.

The interlude soon ended, and the chauffeur drove us back to our hotel. We were leaving in a couple of days, and my mother had been told of the economic austerity under which the British were suffering. She wanted to outfit us with clothes suitable for the cool, wet climate, because rationing in England would limit the number of clothes we could buy there. Although I now hate shopping, that was a fun expedition. The stores were packed with happy people. You wouldn't have known that the war with Japan was still going on if it were not for the numerous places where American servicemen were showing pictures or movie clips and demonstrating to support military recruiting or sales of war bonds. My mother bought several suitcases, and we then proceeded to buy enough clothes to fill them.

Back at our hotel, mother arranged the packing so that we would each have one suitcase in our cabin when we boarded the ship to England; the other suitcases would be stowed in the baggage hold. Much to my disappointment, my treasure of artifacts stuffed into the artillery shell was relegated to one of the suitcases that would go in the hold.

∞ ∞ ∞

On the morning of our departure, the chauffeur picked us up in his limousine and took us to the dock. When we arrived, I stood in awe looking up at the huge liner we were about to board. Like the *John Lykes*, it was painted battleship gray, but it was so much larger that it made the *John Lykes* look like a toy. We were to board the *Ile de France*, one of the luxury superliners that raced across the Atlantic between Europe and America before the war. After France surrendered to the Germans, the British took her over and converted her to a troopship.

The *Ile de France*, like the other fast liners such as the *Queen Elizabeth* and *Queen Mary*, did not cross the Atlantic in convoys during the war. They relied on their exceptional speed to outrun the submarine wolf packs that lay in wait for the convoys, zigzagging to mask their true course. With the war now ended in Europe, our voyage was to have the distinction of being the first to cross the Atlantic without taking evasive action, speeding our trip by a day or more.

The passenger manifest was a combination of troops and civilians. Again, I was separated from my mother and sister and shared a cabin with 11 other young men and boys. We had a large cabin that must have been a luxury suite in the prewar days, but now had six double-deck bunks. Our dining room was separate from the military one, and we sat at real tables and chairs, serving ourselves from a buffet. This was definitely an upgrade from our former troop ship, like moving from coach to first class on a modern airline.

We were under way in the late afternoon. Once the *Ile de France* cleared the congestion outside the harbor, the boilers were fired up for more steam, enough to make 25 knots on a heading northeast into the Atlantic along the great circle route that was the shortest distance to the Irish Sea. A cold wind chilled us as we sailed the same patch of the North Atlantic where the *Titanic* had met its doom after hitting an iceberg.

My years in the tropics had conditioned me for hot weather, and as the temperature on deck was chilled by the wind, mist, and rain, I was extremely uncomfortable. Some passengers wrapped in blankets huddled on deck chairs. I spent little time topside, choosing to take shelter below deck. The ship was built in the days before stabilizers, and the rough weather kept it in constant motion. Though I was never sea sick, I was ill at ease, and would have been much better off had I spent more time on deck where I could fix the horizon and learn to move with the motion. Despite this, the voyage went quickly, and all I missed were more opportunities to stuff myself with the fine food.

We were about a day away from England when we got word that a rogue German submarine had been operating in the area. It had failed to identify its position and return to the nearest port, as directed under the terms of the surrender. Now there was fear it would strike one final blow for the fatherland in vicious retribution for the shame of the surrender. The *Ile de France* took evasive maneuvers, which delayed our arrival by half a day.

Before dawn on the day of our arrival, I put on all of the warm clothes I could find and went to the bow of the ship. I loved to see a ship's approach to land, and despite the chilly morning, wasn't going to miss this one. As the sky brightened in the east, the hills of Scotland were silhouetted, becoming increasingly clear as the sun rose. Surrounded by low islands, we entered the Firth of Clyde, home of some of the largest ship-yards in the world, including the one that had built the *Queen Elizabeth*, at the time the largest ship afloat.

We slowly made our way up river and soon docked in Greenoch, the port for Glasgow. The approach did not seem as impossibly long as it had when we landed in Los Angeles. As we slid by the hills, I got my first impression of Scotland.

Upstate New York had been incredibly green in its spring foliage, but the green of Scotland seemed infinitely brighter. The explanation was clear—from the gray sky fell a steady light drizzle, which was the normal weather pattern here, unless it was really raining.

We disembarked and in the customs shed located the baggage that we had checked into the hold. The suitcase in which I had packed my treasures of souvenirs seemed rather light, so I opened it. To my dismay, my artillery shell filled with cartridge casings and shrapnel was gone. I was devastated. It was all I had to show for three and one-half years in Manila, aside from a lot of bad memories. I learned then that the dockworkers in New York were exceptionally corrupt and helped themselves to whatever took their fancy in the passengers' luggage. The unusual weight of the suitcase was probably a clue that it held something of exceptional interest.

We took a taxi to the Glasgow railroad station and soon were on our way south. As the old steam locomotive chugged slowly out of the station and through an industrial area, it became quite clear that Britain had not been spared by the war. It is one thing to read or hear about the Blitz, it is quite another to see the results, and they were abundant here—buildings reduced to rubble and gaping holes in the sides of others. The Germans had viciously bombed harbors and industrial sites all over Britain.

We soon traversed the little over 100 miles to Carlisle, traveling through incredibly green and gently rolling hills. The station had changed little from when we had left almost seven years earlier, its soaring steel girder-supported glass roof still intact. This corner of England had little industry and was spared the might of the German air armadas.

My grandparents met us at the station. After an emotional reunion, we climbed into my grandfather's venerable Lanchester car and headed for their home. In the distance, I saw the foreboding structure of the Garlands Institute for the Insane, and was surprised that we drove past the turnoff to the gate. My grandfather had retired and now lived in the small village of Whetheral, a short distance down the road.

We turned through a gate onto a gravel parkway in front of a comfortable looking two-story stone house, my home for the next two years. I had come full circle, completely circumnavigating the globe and experiencing many an adventure along the way. The war with Japan was still being fought fiercely in the Pacific, but here, in a tranquil corner of the globe, I could begin a normal childhood. But little did I know that the vestiges of war were not yet finished with me, and more ordeals awaited.

TWENTY THREE

JAPAN SURRENDERS

The village of Whetheral was typically English, with about 40 homes scattered around a village green and supported by a small general store-post office, one pub, and a small hotel. Located in the northwest of England near the Scottish border, Whetheral was probably the most beautiful place I have ever lived. Perched on a wooded bluff above the River Eden, it would have been paradise except for the snake that was the weather. In the first year I lived there, it rained sometime during the day on all but six days.

My grandparents' home was on the corner where the main road from Carlisle terminated and across from the village green. It was a large property with two enormous cedar trees in the front, one on each side of a lush lawn, and an enormous backyard with a huge vegetable garden rampant with berry bushes and fruit trees. Once, an iron fence surrounded the property, but sometime during the war, someone used a torch to cut the iron palings so the fence could be reprocessed into bombs and tanks. Now only the rusty stubs of the fence remained sticking out of the concrete base.

On the far side of the village green, the road plunged steeply down the bluff to end at the river. Halfway down, a sandstone Norman church nestled in a grove of trees, with ancient gravestones leaning at odd angles in the dank dirt and uncut grass and weeds. Inside the church narrow arched windows filled with stained glass filtered the sunlight. Below them were crypts of ancient knights, their likeness carved in the stone of the lid.

The River Eden was wide, deep, and clear running, fed by the frequent rains in the Pennines, the hills that were the backbone of England. Across the river on a bluff stood an old sandstone castle. For a few pennies, the ferryman would row me across, and I would climb the steep path to the plateau above, then walk a mile and recross the river on the high arching railroad viaduct. Along our side of the river were walking paths through thick woods. Hiking upstream, I would wind up at caves carved into the sandstone cliff by some long-forgotten monks. It was rumored that the princes who owned the castle across the river had built an escape tunnel under the river to these caves, but no one had ever found it. Instead, the caves now seemed to be used as public toilets.

From the caves, a steep trail wound down to the river where a wide bench of rock extended well out into the water. Here was my favorite swimming place. I could dive into the deep water at the edge of the shelf and swim underwater, meeting salmon that inhabited the clear water. The River Eden was well named for its garden-like natural beauty. For me, it was a wonderful place to recover from the rigors of Santo Tomas.

∞ ∞ ∞

Despite living in this idyllic place, I was extremely aware that England continued to suffer from the austerity forced by the war. Her troops were occupying German territory and were still fighting the Japanese in Asia. For all intents, the war had bankrupted England's treasury and destroyed a significant portion of her industry and cities.

Everything was rationed, from bread to clothing, and even electricity was turned off for portions of every day. When Americans complained about rationing, they didn't even come close to the deprivation that the British suffered. To add insult to injury, the islands were sinking under the weight of American forces, whose lowest ranked soldier earned in excess of what even the British professionals were paid. They had money to burn, and threw it around like big spenders in the pubs, restaurants, and places of entertainment in the towns and villages near their bases. The garbage cans at their bases were filled with wholesome food that was completely unattainable for their hosts. With money and access to food and luxury goods, American troops cut a wide swath through the young women, who were especially vulnerable because a large number of British men were serving overseas.

Though the British resented these aspects of the American presence, there was never any doubt that they admired Americans, welcomed the troops, and appreciated all that America had done and was doing in pursuing the war. Though they seldom expressed any resentment to Americans, the British had a jocular saying among themselves: "There are only three things wrong with the Americans. They're overpaid, over-sexed, and over here." After the war, hundreds of thousands of British girls left for America as war brides. On the home front, an explosion of births served as testament to the passing American presence.

In my grandparents home, we lived a life typical for the British middle class under the austere conditions. There were six of us, my grandparents, my mother, sister and I, and the cook/housekeeper Lizzie Blenkinsop. Lizzie was what had to be considered a salt-of-the-earth Cumbrian, though her accent had been tempered over the years by her household service. She was as wide as she was tall, ran the household with a firm hand, and could do wonders with the poor fare we provided for meals. I spent many an hour in her enormous kitchen with its coal burning stove, sampling the magical delicacies she produced and listening to her North Country wisdom.

Practically everything we bought required a peek at our ration books to see if we had enough points to cover the purchase. We seldom had an egg. We were lucky to get one a week. Meat was rationed to a few ounces per week. My grandparents pooled all of our ration books to buy a weekly "joint" of meat for Sunday dinner, which may as well have been from a worked-to-death horse as beef, mutton, or pork. We existed the rest of the week on leftovers, or fish and cheese, which were more plentiful. Vegetables were also plentiful, and fruit when it was in season. By American standards, it was a spartan fare, but it was healthy, and we began to rebuild our bodies from the Santo Tomas ordeal.

∞ ∞ ∞

We closely followed the reports on the progress of the war in the Pacific and East Asia, where my father was now serving as a liaison officer at Chiang Kai Shek's headquarters in Chungking. Everywhere, people talked about the impending invasion of Japan, when and where it would happen. Underlying the conversations were concerns about the casualty toll the battle would exact. Some people hinted that it would be so difficult to defeat the Japanese on their home islands that the Allies would suffer more casualties than they already had in the preceding six years of fighting. There was a mixed elation at how rapidly the Japanese armies were collapsing in the occupied countries and foreboding about how the entire population of Japan would be organized to push back the invaders. The stories of the recent invasion of Okinawa with its Japanese population were cited as just a taste of the total resistance that could be expected.

On my tenth birthday, August 13, 1945, the Emperor of Japan, unbeknown to me, gave the one gift I could never have hoped to have. Across the International Date Line it was August 14 when the Emperor broadcast a message to the Japanese people that he was accepting the Potsdam Declaration, which was essentially a call for unconditional surrender. On August 15, 1945, President Harry Truman accepted the surrender and announced that the war was over.

In the small village of Whetheral, everyone was smiling and congratulating each other. That evening a raucous celebration at the pub, which was clear on the other side of the village from where I lived, kept me awake until very late. I was happy too, but with a mixed state of wonder. Like everyone else, I'd expected the war to go on for another two years and hoped for a highly publicized bloody defeat of the Japanese.

Radio newscasts about the new weapon that led to Japan's complete capitulation began to filter in. To my ears, the newscasters were talking about a fearsome thing called the "A-tonic" bomb. It wasn't until a few days later, when we attended the cinema in Carlisle, that I saw how atomic bombs completely annihilated both Hiroshima and Nagasaki.

I think back now about my feelings when I saw film of the devastation and heard about the high number of casualties. I felt neither elation nor sorrow. The Japanese killed tens of millions of people, many in such a horrific way that it defied imagination. Here on the screen was the symbol of retribution. The death of a couple of hundred thousand Japanese could hardly repay the misery that Japan had visited on East Asia. The film was graphic, showing burned corpses lying on the streets and in gutted buildings. But then, when I compared it with the devastation of Manila, where more Filipinos died than Japanese at Hiroshima, I could not feel much sympathy. I could lay pictures of Hiroshima next to pictures of Manila and see little difference in the leveling of these two cities.

Today it has become fashionable for Americans to decry the use of the atomic weapons on civilian populations in 1945, and to march in protests on the anniversary. Those well-fed free protestors have no idea how gruesome the war already was until the United States stepped forward to end it with one quick brutal blow before it could consume the lives of millions more. It is only when you have the historical perspective to understand the depth of agony and fear that existed, the huge toll of lives, and the prospect for continuing conflict that you can rationally evaluate why President Truman authorized dropping two atomic bombs.

The war was over, but the consequences were yet to be faced because it had spawned more conflicts. The iron curtain slammed down across Germany and Eastern Europe, starting the cold war, and hot wars were heating up in Palestine and China.

My family was spread half a world apart, and my mother and father would now have to plan how they would put their lives back together. I presumed that since the war was over, my father would no longer be needed at Chiang Kai Shek's headquarters, and we could re-establish our lives in China. As it turned out, my mother and sister would leave for China the next spring, but I was doomed to remain in England. I had my own little war yet to fight, and one more big adventure.

TWENTY FOUR

AN END TO WAR'S ODYSSEY

Since leaving China four years ago, I had missed almost two years of schooling. It was now time to pay the piper. I was enrolled in Lime House, an English grammar school just across the green from my grandparent's home. For the autumn term in 1945 and winter term in 1946, I was a day student. In the spring of 1946, after my mother and sister left for China, I became a boarding student.

This was a whole new world, especially when I became a boarding student with all of the discipline and restrictions imposed on me. To this day, I'm not sure which was worse, Santo Tomas or Lime House. To start with, the English curricula was much more stringent than the American, which I had been following when a prisoner. At my grade level, the English students were studying Latin and French, algebra and geometry, subjects of which I had no inkling.

Discipline was harsh with no room for infractions of the rules. The extreme punishment was a caning by the head master. Other public humiliations were handed out for lesser infractions. Some of the masters, as the teachers were called, were sadistic and took it out on me because they perceived me as an American and an easy target. For example, the English spell differently from the Americans, and in my first spelling test, I spelled only 22 out of 50 words correctly. I suspect that the master deliberately selected words for the test that highlighted the differences. I had learned to write in a cursive script, but the English demanded that everything be printed. And so the differences continued, keeping me off balance for quite awhile, until I finally caught on.

I had long since mastered my old nemesis, long division, and found it relatively easy to catch up with my class in algebra and geometry. Latin was a horrendous problem for me. I was at least three years behind my class. Learning the mysteries of conjugating Latin verbs seemed a hopeless and useless exercise. I was also well behind my classmates in French. It soon became clear to me, if not to my family, that I would never catch up in time to qualify to enter a good English prep school.

Though academically I was a bit of a bust, socially I got along well. With my American accent, I was considered a bit exotic, because the British were fascinated with the American GIs who had swarmed across their island during the fighting in Europe. The social system in the school, which had a little over 50 students, was strictly hierarchical. The older and bigger boys dominated the younger and smaller. I was in the upper level of age and about medium in size, so in the one sense I was part of the dominant group and the other I was in the dominated. Though I was small for my age, and still relatively weak, I was tough and resisted bullying and soon earned the respect that allowed me to fit into my proper place in the social hierarchy.

∞ ∞ ∞

In 1946, following the spring term when I boarded at school, I moved back to my grandparents' home for the summer break. I had plenty of company to keep me occupied. The son of the headmaster at Lime House was about my age, and I had made friends with a couple of the village boys. In addition, my grandparents must have wanted some peace and quiet without me, so they arranged trips for me to visit my uncles.

My first trip that summer was to visit Uncle Ronald and Aunt Bunty in Liverpool. Ronald was still the happy go lucky man that I had grown to love before the war, so a visit to his home was always a treat. Their two boys, the twins as the family called them, were both away. John was a seaman in the Royal Navy and his ship was on a deployment to the China Sea. Peter was an officer with the Scots Guards serving on occupation duty in Germany.

Usually, Uncle Ronald would turn me loose during the day to explore Liverpool on my own. On one of my forays, I wound up at the Mersey River near where my family had left for China right after the war started in 1939. The Germans had targeted the docks for destruction in their blitz to stop the flow of ships that was Britain's lifeline during the war. Many buildings and docks were reduced to rubble, but the port was still operating as if everything were normal, while work crews cleared away the destruction in preparation for rebuilding.

Another trip took me to visit Uncle Ian and my cousins in southern England. They lived in Beaconsfield, a beautiful village in the Thames Valley in the middle of wooded country. We spent a lot of time exploring and playing games in the woods. We also took day trips into London.

The city had not yet recovered from the war, and the bright lights of the theater district and Piccadilly Circus were dark. Moving around the city, I'd see a light flow of taxis and double-decker buses, but few cars, with many pedestrians staunchly going about their business completely oblivious to the destruction around them. We could go down a street and see a perfectly normal city, then turn a corner and see several blocks that had been flattened during the blitz or by one of the deadly V-bombs. The V-1—what the English called a buzz bomb—could be heard coming because of the noise of its ramjet engine. When the noise stopped, everyone ducked for cover. The V-2 was a ballistic missile, and there was no warning before it struck. Both bombs were inaccurate. The Germans simply aimed them in the general direction of London, where they destroyed and killed on a completely random basis.

Seeing the destruction in Glasgow when we first arrived, then during this summer seeing the results of the bombing in Liverpool and London, and thinking of the toll of lives, made me realize that many others had shared the misery through which I'd lived.

∞ ∞ ∞

The summer was soon over, and I returned to Lime House. Life became routine again. I dreaded the day that I would have to move on to a prep school because I felt so inadequate in my studies. Then news arrived from my parents. The Chinese Communists, who had been well armed by the Russians when the war ended, were now rolling down from the north in China, defeating the Nationalists in battle after battle. The handwriting was on the wall, China was going to fall to the Communists as so many European countries had after the war. It was no place for my family to live.

My father decided that our family could not remain in China under a Communist regime. He retired from American Asiatic Underwriters and took a position with the parent company, AIU, in San Francisco. In January 1947, my father, mother, and sister set sail from Shanghai. At the end of the school year in England, I would join them. Now I could really look forward to something new.

∞ ∞ ∞

At summer break in 1947, I left Lime House with few regrets. Another year there and I'd have had to start learning Greek, which would have been a challenge since Latin and French were already Greek to me. When the spring term ended, I waved goodbye to my friends for the last time and didn't look back.

I had received an American passport, and it seemed strange to me that just as I was beginning to feel British again, I had become definitively American. However, in the last two years, I had mostly replaced my American accent with an English one, so once I reached America, I'd again be considered British. I had a choice: either be confused by my constant alien status or try to take advantage of it. After reaching America, though, I soon discovered that Americans didn't share the same extreme fascination with Brits that the Brits showed for the Americans.

Later, when I started high school, I started to hang around with a group of Nisei boys. Other students would ask why I was associating with the "Japanese," but to me they were simply Americans, and I was pleased to be accepted as a friend. We had little in common except being the same age and the tie of having being imprisoned during the war, albeit under very different circumstances. But their families had made sacrifices too, and many of their fathers, uncles, and brothers had served in the famous 442nd Regimental Combat Team, the most decorated unit in the U.S. Army. Like me, they were not yet accepted in the mainstream of American society, so we had an affinity for each other.

In late July 1947, I boarded the train for the all-day trip to London and caught the boat train to Southampton. Again Uncle Ronald had worked his magic, this time getting me passage on the *Queen Elizabeth*, the flagship of the Cunard Line, and the biggest passenger ship afloat. He had also arranged to place me under the guidance of one of his friends who was going to New York on business. He laughingly informed me that I didn't have to worry about anyone harassing us because his friend was the man who had given Herman Göring the potassium cyanide that he used to commit suicide. Göring was one of the highest officials in the Nazi party, was Hitler's appointed successor, and was the architect of the "Final Solution" for the execution of the Jews. Sentenced to death during the Nüremberg war crimes trials, he poisoned himself just two hours before his scheduled hanging.

The *Queen Elizabeth,* recently converted from wartime troopship service back to a luxury liner, was beautiful. The great ship pulled away from the dock in the late afternoon, and as we sailed westward between the Isle of Wight and the English mainland, we passed the inbound *Queen Mary*. She was completing her sea trials after conversion from being a troopship. This was the first time in eight years that the two ships could be seen together in the splendor of their colorful civilian glory. Aircraft flew overhead as photographers vied for pictures to post in the great London newspapers.

It was a smooth and enjoyable five-day trip across the Atlantic. The most memorable part was the dining room, resplendent in white linen with gleaming crystal and silver, and attentive service. That of course did not impress me. What did was the food. During our brief stay in America in 1945, we had dined very well, but the fare in England during the next two years had been mediocre at best. Now we dined on the best that the world could supply in unlimited portions. I took advantage of the largesse and started the slow transition from a wiry frame to a chubby one that was characteristic of my first three years in America.

∞ ∞ ∞

Early on the morning we reached New York, I was on deck to catch my first sign of land. Many others were on deck by the time we entered the harbor and sailed past the Statue of Liberty. What a wonderful symbol of America she was. I looked around at the other passengers. Many had tears in their eyes. Most of them had close ties to America or were citizens returning home after an extended stay in Europe during and after the war. It was an emotional moment for all of us.

By mid morning, I walked down the gangway with Ronald's infamous friend, who had turned out to be a lot of fun and very accommodating to my whims. After we passed through immigration, we discovered my brother John waiting nearby on the dock. My escort was probably delighted with the opportunity to finally hand off his difficult charge.

John was still tall and handsome in his civilian clothes. Only an instant, it seemed, had passed since I last saw him, leaving us in our New York hotel to take the train back to Washington, D.C., to resume his duties with the Army.

∞ ∞ ∞

When the war ended, John took his discharge in Washington, DC, and remained in the area, marrying a local girl. They now had a newborn son and were living in Falls Church, Virginia. The plan was for me to return with him to his home and then take an airline flight to San Francisco. We took a taxi to Grand Central Station and from there a train to Washington. By evening, we were at his home, and I was introduced to his wife, Betty, and their son, John Dare Lorenzen II.

I spent the day visiting, and in the evening, John drove me to Washington National Airport, where I boarded a United Airlines DC-6 for the flight across the United States. For 14 hours the plane droned across the continent, landing at the San Francisco airport in the morning. I climbed down the stairs from the airplane and walked across the tarmac to the terminal. I soon spotted my mother and sister among a crowd of people waiting at the entrance to the building. My father, who I hadn't seen for what literally was half of my lifetime, was with them. He was older than I remembered, still big and hearty, but now a little stooped. The war had not been kind to him.

My father had tears in his eyes as he bent to give me a hug and a kiss. This embarrassed me no end. I would have preferred to shake his hand in greeting since the British school experience had beaten any sign of emotion out of me. Perhaps it was that combined with my experience in Santo Tomas that left me with an emotional void. But I endured the moment, and even hugged him back. It felt really good to be back with my family.

My parents had bought a small home in San Mateo, about 17 miles south of San Francisco. The Japanese, who had taken our home in Tientsin and everything in it, had wiped out my parents financially. Oh yes, there was a War Claims Commission that would evaluate claims against the Japanese government and repay at least a part of them from the war reparations that the U.S. government extracted from the Japanese. But settling the claims wouldn't happen until 20 years in the future. My father had reclaimed the silver that his major domo, Liu Lau, had smuggled from our home in Tientsin under the noses of the Japanese. The proceeds from the sale of some of it provided a little capital. My mother had a small inheritance from an aunt, and that, along with the proceeds from the silver, is what they used for the down payment on their new home. Meanwhile, my father commuted into San Francisco by bus to work in the AIU office on Sansome Street. They lived a simple, thrifty life on a modest income, but my father never again achieved the status and wealth of his prewar life.

Even though the war was over, its effects haunted my parents for the rest of their lives. My father died the year before the War Claims Commission finally distributed its hoard. By then, inflation had eaten away more than half its value. But that really didn't matter because the Commission refused to make the payment to my mother, though she legally inherited my father's estate, using the excuse that she was a British citizen and therefore not qualified for compensation. And so my lovely little war finally ended, leaving my parents financially devastated, the pecuniary consequences being equally as bad as anything that physically happened to us.

But I was young, just 12 years old, and kids are resilient and I had a full life ahead of me. Life has been more than generous to make up for those few bad years. But I no longer look at war with those same innocent child's eyes, for battles aren't fought by little lead soldiers. It is so clear to me that it isn't just armies that suffer and die, but the innocent populations caught between the grindstones. For them, the war isn't over when the battle ceases, but lingers and changes their lives forever.

EPILOGUE

I remained in the San Francisco Bay Area for ten years, until I graduated from the University of California with a Bachelor of Science in engineering. Then I moved to Southern California, where I went to work for an international engineering and construction company. I remained with the company for most of my career, winding up as Vice President of Engineering. When I retired, my wife and I remained in the home we had built high on that same hill overlooking San Pedro that had been my first glimpse of America when repatriated from Manila.

In all of those years, my experience in the war became more deeply suppressed in my mind and was inconsequential in guiding my life. Some people may beg to differ with that statement, but aside from being tough-minded and somewhat introverted, I can't think of a single trait that can be directly attributed to my years as a prisoner. Children are amazingly resilient, and with an effective support mechanism, can endure things that would destroy an adult.

In recent years, I have become active in the support group for civilian ex-POWs. For years, there was no such group. People were told when they were liberated that they had to reintegrate into society and get on with their lives. Most people did that as best they could, putting out of their minds any memories of the horrifying experience they had survived. Post-tramatic stress disorder hadn't been invented yet, and those who suffered nightmares or failed to reintegrate with society, received no counseling or assistance. They were told to "suck it up" and get on with life.

During World War II, over 14,000 Americans were held in Japanese prison camps throughout Asia. Those who remain today are primarily the children and young adults. They are finally coming out of the shell of silence that has characterized so much of their lives. They gather at our reunions and talk more freely about their own experiences. Their descendents also attend and listen in awe, often with tears in their eyes. They never realized the deprivation their parents had endured, and some were completely unaware that their parents had been prisoners because they were never told.

My sister is one who maintained an aura of silence, and though her children knew she had been a prisoner, they knew nothing about it. Recently her children have become interested and attend the reunions, drawing her along with them, so she finally has accepted that phase of her life. After a recent reunion she commented to me that, if we hadn't been in Santo Tomas, we would never have learned to do anything for ourselves. We would have lived lives of privilege, catered by a bevy of servants. But the war changed that, and we became self-sufficient, resilient people.

It wasn't until 1997 that I returned to Santo Tomas. That brief one-day visit whetted my appetite to better understand what had happened there. When I noticed a bulletin about a 60th anniversary celebration tour to the Philippines in 2005, I immediately subscribed. Our tour group included ex-prisoners from Santo Tomas and Los Baños, military members of the flying column, and ex-POWs captured on Bataan and Corregidor. We followed the route of the Death March, visited the Cabanatuan and Camp O'Donnell POW camps, toured the site of the internment camp at Los Baños where so many of our friends had been sent, and visited the Intramuros which has been mostly rebuilt since its horrible destruction. This broadened my understanding of all that had happened around me in that period from December 1941 to April 1945.

The highlight of the tour was a full day at Santo Tomas, again a thriving university with more than 40,000 students. Here, we 15 ex-prisoners and invited guests at Santo Tomas were the stars. We explained the horrifying events that had occurred in and around their beloved campus to the students and faculty, who had little knowledge of what happened here. When they questioned us, we pointed to the patches over the Japanese shelling damage in the Main Building that they had never noticed, nor did they know about the people killed by those blasts in the very classrooms they were still using.

People ask me how the Filipinos feel today about the Japanese who inflicted such pain on them. In my discussions with these younger people, I noted no animosity, and in fact, very little knowledge of what happened. To them, the battle of Manila was as remote in history as the American Civil War was to me when I was in school. History does have a wonderful way of healing battle scars, and, as has been said, "he who was my enemy is now my friend."

Older people gave me the best perspective. The speakers at the liberation celebration, including the American Ambassador, a Philippine state senator, and the university president, all touched on one theme, "Through the generations, we must remember what happened here." However, the most succinct comment I heard was from Diosdado Guaytingco, the guerilla who had carried his dying leader onto the campus on the night of liberation, and now in his 80s still an active attorney. He said: "We can finally forgive the Japanese for what they did, but we must never forget."

Diosdado Guaytingco, the first Filipino guerilla to enter Santo Tomas on the night of liberation, and Angus Lorenzen meet and share stories at the 60th anniversary.

INDEX